Life Bytes:
Growing Up Geek

Part One
The New Frontier

For Ronnie, who played video games with me while I grew up.
And for Trey, who I play video games with while he grows up.

Table of Contents

Foreword

As a game creator whose career took off in the 1980s, it is wonderful to read the account of these same times from the eyes of a player. In these days, long before the internet, creators like myself had no idea what players might actually be thinking and experiencing as they played our games. All we could go on was sales, and the occasional 'fan mail', which was often more of a 'Hey, let me tell you how to make your game better!' communique.

So it was with great pleasure that I read Kristian Bland's account of Growing Up Geek, as it is the other side of our shared story. A story that would not only shape our lives, but shape an entire industry. That industry today is now unquestionably the dominant form of global media. But herein, you can find one person's path through these formative times in life and this new medium.

Enjoy!

-Richard "Lord British" Garriott
Creator of the Ultima series and onward through Shroud of the Avatar

Introduction

NOTE: *This book was originally much more comprehensive than it ended up being. Coming in around 800 pages long, there was no way I could publish it independently without having to charge way more than anyone would ever be willing to pay, so I'm dividing it up over three books, each one representing a number of years in my life and the games I was playing at the time. The one you're reading right now covers not only my early years as a small human, but the early years of gaming itself. I was lucky enough to grow up alongside this amazing, ridiculous industry, and this book is for others who did the same thing. It's also for all the people who weren't lucky enough to be there at the dawn of gaming and want to know what it was like. Nostalgia for some and a history lesson for others. I'll try not to be boring.*

I grew up in the Deep South. Specifically, in a small city in Southeast Texas called Beaumont, and there really isn't anything more to say about it. Instead, I'm going to talk for a minute about what life in the Deep South does to people. Or, rather, what it did to me growing up.

The first and most important thing you need to understand is that everything is pastiche in the Deep South. This is because nothing is really real in any way that matters. Take seasons, for example. The South doesn't have them. The leaves never change color in the fall, snow never falls in the winter, the entirety of spring consists of about half a dozen nice days that serve as a warning that summer is coming, and then...summer comes. Most of the year is summer, with a few days of other seasons sprinkled in just to tease you.

Where the pastiche comes in is in how everyone in the South *pretends* they experience actual seasons. There are no harvests here, apart from whenever it is that you harvest rice and soybeans. There are festivals for that, but it's hard to get too worked up about piles of white grains in the same way one can get excited for, say, pumpkins. The South does have pumpkin patches in the fall, though. It's just that

Christmas in the South

they're usually on the front lawns of churches and they're filled with pumpkins grown someplace else, imported and then plopped down amid scattered hay bales to give the impression of a fall harvest.

The same goes for winter. It never snows, but all around are decorations and homes dolled up in snowflakes and snowmen and all the usual Christmastime trappings. Even when the weather doesn't dip below the mid-70s (on many Christmas mornings, you can drive around and see kids riding around on their brand new bicycles while wearing shorts and t-shirts), you'll still find people dressed up in whatever the latest winter fashions are for any given year. Designed for actual cold weather, the people wearing them might sweat and stink, but they look fabulous.

Even the summer - the time of year that most permeates every waking hour in the Deep South - is an echo of what it's supposed to be. What it's *expected* to be. The temperature regularly climbs well over 100 degrees and stays there, day and night, while the humidity is always - always - so thick and heavy that it threatens to suffocate anyone who dares go outdoors. People not from the South don't really understand the whole humidity thing, but my kid used to think it was tree sweat - which isn't nearly as goofy as it sounds from an 8-year-old's perspective. Trees are, after all, always outdoors where it's hot and miserable, so they must be sweating their barks off. Makes sense, especially when you consider the smell. And yet, all of the usual images of summer are there. Spending time outside, frolicking in the green grass among the rolling hills that don't exist, kids all smiles as they run and play and experience nature - all of these things are just marketing. In reality, the Southern sun is trying to kill us all, and what it can't manage on its own, the mosquitoes and snakes are more than happy to take care of.

Everything is pretend in the South. People make up stories about how the Civil War wasn't actually about slavery, not really, even though everyone knows it was. People invent alternative histories where the South somehow has some, but it's not like other places that have old castles and mansions or ancient burial grounds. Nothing really lives in the bones of the geography here. Everything only exists in the now, and everything in the now is a copy of something that happens someplace else.

Which, I think, is why I am the way that I am. Why I found my place inside books and movies and video games. Everything in all the fictions I threw myself into might have been fake, but books and games were at least honest about it. Watching everyone go through the motions and engage in some kind of weird, collective delusion every season was not only unsettling, it was just plain annoying. Everyone was always pretending they were somewhere else and someone else, and I wanted nothing to do with it.

And so, I dove into my fantasies and never came up for air. I lost myself in the word-worlds of Tolkien and Pratchett, in the visual splendor of Lucas and Spielberg, and in the interactive realities of Garriott and Gilbert and Miyamoto. Each book I read took me to another place, where I could escape the bizarre simulacrum of the South and slip into a reality that was more real to me than anything my actual world had to offer.

The land of Britannia became a second home to me, the characters of each Ultima weren't just my companions in the game; they were my friends. Every moment I spent inside their world felt like home. Each new day outside of it was torture. Kids were mean, I didn't like the things they liked, and I didn't buy into the consensus fiction everyone around me seemed lost in. But in my books and my movies and my games, I created my own worlds.

Sure, I was just reading the words Tolkien had written, but in a way, they were just a road map. A guide to conjuring Middle Earth in my own head, to look the way I wanted it to look. To feel the way I wanted it to feel. The same was true with Britannia. The crudely animated stick figures became mighty warriors and terrible wizards in my imagination. The little blobs of green that dotted the landscape became dense forests filled with terrors. My games didn't try to convince me they were real, not in the same way vinyl snowflakes slapped on a window tried to convince me it was winter. Instead, they were more of a portal - an opening I could push through to get to something real on the other side, which was always in my head.

The early days of gaming were defined by experimentation. Developers were making and breaking all the rules with every new title they released. The games were weird and wonderful and always demanded more from the player than they were able to provide, creating a kind of symbiosis between man and machine. The computer provided the rough outlines. The player filled in the fine details. Imagination was key, and the early games exploited that to the fullest effect.

Gaming was also something I did with my dad, which you'll find out more about as you read through this book. It was a shared hobby between generations, something new for both of us, and as we figured out how to solve puzzles and vanquish evil foes, we were also learning how to navigate the ups and downs of the father-son relationship. Playing games with my dad taught me holding on to childlike wonder well into adulthood was a good thing, and they showed me that it was okay to be a weirdo.

This book is about all of that and a little more. I hope you enjoy it.

Growing Up Geek

In the present day, photorealistic video games featuring alternate realities and fully realized artificial worlds line the shelves of game stores everywhere. I can start up a game, hop online and kill, shoot, stab, beat, maim, assassinate, decapitate, dismember and in all other ways straight up murder friends and strangers around the world. I can log in to an MMO and live a virtual life as a fearsome orc or a noble hunter in a mystical realm filled with magic and wonder and plenty of fetch quests. With modern advances in graphics, connectivity, and raw computing power, it's never been a better time to be a gamer.

Which is why I've been playing a lot of games lately.

With bad graphics.

And limited gameplay.

From the '80s and '90s and early 2000s.

Why? Because life is a constant struggle and growing up was a trap, which is why this book is about what I do to cope with the awful reality of living in a world that seems hell-bent on bludgeoning you to death with the hammer of bureaucracy and the sickle of injustice.

And what I do is play video games.

Old video games.

From when I was a kid and life didn't suck.

Some people watch old movies or listen to music that strikes the right

Yep, that's me with an epic +10 Bowl Cut.

nostalgia-soaked power chords of their youth, but I turn instead to the games I played growing up. For whatever reason, whether it's because they're interactive or they take longer to experience, or just because playing them is what I spent most of my time doing when I was a kid, games massage my nostalgia gland like nothing else can. I boot up an old computer game and I'm instantly whisked back to an age where I spent most of my free time sitting at an old desk in my childhood bedroom, using a computer to transport me to fantastic worlds of myths and monsters and pirates.

Although I didn't know it at the time, life was simpler then. My days might have been filled with the intolerable miseries of a public school education, but my nights were open to flights of fantasy, with the computer as my portal to strange new worlds. Whether I became an Avatar of the eight virtues in Britannia or a scrawny smart aleck with delusions of swashing his buckle like a really real pirate somewhere deep in the Caribbean, gaming took me to places I'd never been. It allowed me to escape the emo-drenched courtyards and angst-ridden pathways of a teenager growing up in the '80s, but there was more to it than that. I may play them *now* to escape an increasingly bizarre reality, but I played them *then* to explore. Long before I discovered the twisted (and honest) worlds created by writers with names like Ellison, Gaiman, Pratchett, and Thompson, I was charting the weird and wonderful landscapes of game designers like Ron Gilbert, Tim Schafer and Richard Garriott.

But it wasn't just games. I also spent a lot of time dialing into local Bulletin Board Systems with, at first, a 300 baud modem on an Apple 2 that appeared under the tree one Christmas morning. Later, I'd eventually graduate to a 1200 baud modem, then a 2400, then a 9600, 14.4k, 28.8k...all the way up to high-speed broadband and, eventually, the internet. But while I wouldn't trade my always-on connection of today for the hit-or-miss modular handshakes of my youth, I'll never love technology now as much as I loved it then, during those early days of posting to message boards, playing text-based "doors" and chatting with Sysops. Sure, we can do a lot more today when we can transfer data at 20,000,000 bits per second than we could back when just 300 bits were being lazily hand delivered between squawking modems by digital pony express riders, but I don't care. Nostalgia doesn't work like that.

Nostalgia is about dipping into the warm waters of the past, where things are always better than they were and nowhere near as bad as they've become. It's about transporting yourself back to a time when things seemed simpler, even if they weren't. And that's what playing the old games of my youth does for me. When I'm point-and-clicking my way through an old Sierra or Lucasfilm adventure, I don't

```
 Award Modular BIOS v4.51PG, An Energy Star Ally
 Copyright (C) 1984-97, Award Software, Inc.

586TX Ver.C 07/21/1997

PENTIUM-S CPU at 60MHz
Memory Test :   65920K OK

Award Plug and Play BIOS Extension  v1.0A
Copyright (C) 1997, Award Software, Inc.
  Detecting HDD Primary Master  ... None
  Detecting HDD Primary Slave   ... None
  Detecting HDD Secondary Master... None
  Detecting HDD Secondary Slave ... MAME Compressed Hard Disk

Conflict I/O Ports : 2E8 2E8
Floppy disk(s) fail (40)



Press F1 to continue, DEL to enter SETUP
```

remember any of the lousy parts about growing up in a decade defined by parachute pants and voodoo economics; I just remember the good parts. Like finally killing Minax during a quick session of Ultima 2 with my dad one morning before school, or realizing that the red herring in Monkey Island wasn't a red herring at all. Except that it was, and that was the whole point. Either way, I gave the stupid fish to the troll guarding the bridge, which then it took off its mask and turned into George Lucas, proving conclusively that Ron Gilbert can see the future. (This was in 1990, remember. It would take another nine years and the release of The Phantom Menace before the world would discover Lucas' talent for trolling his fans.)

Not that it was all rainbows and moon ponies, though. Far from it. Growing up as a nerd has never been very easy for anyone, but it was particularly difficult for me as a scrawny little nerdchilde in my little east Texas town where the only good game is a football game and the only good book is, well, the Good Book. God, guns, football and the baby Jesus. That's Texas, if you add some cowboy boots and ridiculous hats.

But what made my experience so difficult, or in any way different than that of any nerd growing up anywhere? Well, I did it in the '80s, for a start. Which was a dark time for nerds living in the Bible Belt.

You can't do anything back in my hometown without someone invoking the Holy Spirit in some capacity. Whether it's an opening prayer that repeats the term "Father God" every other word for inexplicable reasons, as if the omnipotent creator of the universe is going to suddenly forget who you're talking to if you don't say his name every few seconds to keep his attention, or maybe a closing prayer, or a mid-whatever prayer, or perhaps just a cautionary explanation from one of your teachers about how science is how the devil gets inside you and you're going to hell for believing in carbon dating. Basically, if you're doing anything in the Deep South, you ain't doin' it without Jesus, boy.

Which made liking fantasy and roleplaying games during the height of the '80s Satanic Panic exceptionally fun.

Playing CRPGs like the Ultima series would, I was warned on innumerable occasions, lead me down a dark path to ritualistic animal sacrifice and drinking blood from the still-beating hearts of virgins if I didn't wise up and change my wicked ways. And don't even think about Dungeons and Dragons, because that combined devil magic with things like math and rolling dice, which was how the demons of Gambling and Reason grabbed hold of the impressionable youth and dragged them off to Hell.

If you were a kid growing up in 1980s Texas and you liked that sort of thing, you had to keep it on the down low. Underground. Keep it secret, sort of thing. Keep it safe.

Even today, as an adult still living in the same timewarp region, people routinely try to make me feel bad about being a nerd. For instance, I made myself a d20 key chain when I was making polyhedral die necklaces for my kid's 8th birthday party years ago. I think it's pretty nifty, but a hyper-local microcelebrity happened to catch a glimpse of it in a picture I posted to Facebook one day, then thought he was being super witty by making a little quip about how *of course* I would have a "D&D dice" key chain. Because being a middle-aged dude with a raging fanboy crush on NASCAR is totally normal around these parts, but rolling dice outside of a nearby Louisiana casino is just plain unnatural.

I've learned to mostly ignore the jibes, and they don't hurt me like they did when I was younger - but they're still annoying. And omnipresent. Like gnats at a picnic.

Getting back to the '80s, I knew a few other nerds growing up. We were friends and all liked some different nerdy thing, but what we all had in common was The Lie.

We all wore masks.

We'd blend in with the "normal" kids as best we could, pretending to give a crap about sports or whatever, or feigning interest in the fad of the day. It was just easier than dealing with the taunts and the bullies, so that's what we did for the English, which is totally what I would've called normal people if I'd known anything about the Amish back before Witness came out.

But for most of my friends - and, I think, most nerds everywhere - that mask of normalcy slowly became permanent. Pretend to be something long enough, and I guess you just eventually forget what you were hiding in the first place. I believe this is commonly referred to as Growing Up.

And it sucks.

We all have to do it, of course. Grow up. But I don't think that has to automatically mean we just stop loving everything we ever enjoyed as children, just so we can convince ourselves that we've matured. Or worse, just so we can convince everyone else that we're adults who like adult things because we're adults. Or something.

With all of this weighing pretty heavily on my mind, I eventually sat down one day and started writing this book of essays strung together into a sort of narrative of my youth as seen through the lens of the games I was playing at the time. Other geek pastimes make an appearance as well, from the BBSs I mentioned to pen-and-paper RPGs and comic books, but it's mostly about the games. And how they've always been there to help get me through whatever nasty surprises life throws my way.

And it's always throwing nasty surprises my way.

Won't someone please think of the children?!

Chapter One

In The Beginning...

I missed the first generation of video games on account of having not been born yet. I blame my parents for that one, and it's a resentment I carry for a few reasons. First, by waiting until 1975 to bring me into the world, they made me miss all the good music of the '60s and most of the '70s.

By the time my ears were my own and I could start choosing what sounds went into them, it was the '80s, which was great if you loved the keytar, but not much good for anything else. Second, Bruce Lee had been dead a full two years before I was finally expelled from my mother's uterus in a lonesome hospital in a little corner of the great state of Texas. And that's no way to come into the world.

Still, my parents did eventually get around to deciding they wanted another kid at some point, or I wouldn't be here. So I'm pretty happy about that, even if I did miss all the best stuff of the past 50 years. Well, except for all the cool stuff of the '80s and early '90s, like computers and lasers and the space shuttle. And video games.

...there was Razzle Dazzle

I was barely five years old when I experienced two moments that would come to define the rest of my life. The second was the premiere of the best movie in the Star Wars franchise, but the first? The first was my introduction to video games.

My dad was working at an electronics shop at the time, and one day he brought home something called the Fairchild Channel F System II

Video Entertainment Computer. I didn't know why it was called that because we didn't have an F channel on our television, but whatever. When you're five years old, you just go with these things.

All these years later, and I still don't know why it was called the Fairchild Channel F System II With The Longest And Worst Product Name Ever System, but I've since concluded that it probably had something to do with the fact that, while the fine minds at Fairchild Semiconductor might have been familiar with the concept of marketing, they never quite got the hang of it.

The only game I remember playing on the thing was a football title called Videocart-24: Pro Football, which stands as another stellar example of the brilliant and creative minds of the Fairchild Semiconductor marketing team. I loved the game, probably because my dad would always play it with me. After all, when you're five years old, all you want to do with your life is whatever your dad is doing with his. And mine was playing video games with me. I loved it.

It was a terrible game though, with lousy graphics and even worse gameplay. I could be wrong here, but in the window of my memory, you didn't actually play much in the way of football when you played Videocart-24. Instead, you just selected something from a list of plays, then watched as the computer ran them. I think you could grab hold of one of the its weird joysticks and push a button to make one X pass a square to another X, but the computer would decide if one of the Os intercepted it. That's how I remember it, anyway.

And I remember the play I always used to run...and when I say that I always used to run it, I mean that I **always** ran it. Every. Single. Time.

It was called Razzle Dazzle, and I thought it sounded really cool. For his part, my Dad never got tired of letting me run the same play over and over again, always acting surprised each and every time he let one of my Xs razzle the holy dazzle out of one of his Os. He did this for two reasons. First, because he was a man of endless patience. And second, because he was a pretty awesome father.

Whenever I try to recall my earliest memories, I always see myself sitting on the hideous 1970s carpet of our family room with a ridiculous controller in my hand and my Dad by my side. We're in front of the TV with our backs to the couch, I'm running Razzle Dazzle again for the 500th time, and my Dad is smiling. And so am I.

Life was perfect.

The Coming of the Wars

Growing up in the '80s meant that Star Wars was not only part of your childhood; in some ways, it *was* your childhood. Sure, the scene in E.T. where Elliot describes his Star Wars toys to the little alien troll

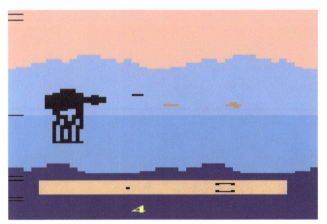

with the phallic neck might have just been a bit of product placement by George Lucas' good buddy Steven Spielberg, but it was also honest. Show me a young boy in the '80s whose world didn't revolve around Han Solo and Luke Skywalker, and I'll show you a religious zealot being home-schooled in the Appalachians, just before he writes a manifesto and blows something up in his underwear. The fact is, if you were a nerdy kid back in the '80s, you dug the 'Wars. End of story.

My first exposure to the saga came about during the re-release of what eventually came to be known as Star Wars: Episode 1: A New Hope. My parents, probably still feeling pretty lousy that Hendrix had been dead and cold for half a decade before they finally got around to creating me, took me to see the film at a local drive-in theater. If you ever went to a drive-in back then, you already know that the experience was pretty great. If, however, you weren't fortunate enough to make it to one before they were all turned into parking lots and driving ranges, it was pretty much the same as going to a movie today. Except that the surround sound was a tiny speaker hooked onto your dad's window (if he was driving), and if the person next to you kept talking throughout the movie, you could just punch her in the arm until she shut up or told on you because she was your sister. In short, drive-ins were awesome. I miss them.

By the time the Empire struck back in 1980, the drive-in was already history and my parents took me to a General Cinema, instead. It had, as I remember, two screens. I don't remember what the other one was showing, because I was only interested in seeing what was going to happen to Luke, Han, and Leia. I won't recount the movie here, but if you're any sort of geek, you'll know that Empire was the best of the series, probably because Lucas had a hard time getting his way with Irvin Kershner. And as the prequels proved, any time no one says, "No!" to George Lucas, a baby Jar-Jar is born.

I lived and breathed Star Wars as a kid, especially after I found out that Vader was Luke's father. (Sorry. Forgot the spoiler warning.) My friends and I would act out the scenes as little boys do, only ours usually ended up more violent than somebody just getting their hand chopped off. I was always careful with my toys, though. I still have most of them, including an original AT-AT (which I never have and never will refer to as a Walker), the Death Star playset, and even a plastic Ewok village. (Yeah, I liked the Ewoks. Fight me.)

I had that one friend though, as everyone does, who didn't give two craps about my toys or their relative safety. Thanks to him, I also have one broken TIE Fighter, two broken X-Wings, and a semi-functional landspeeder with a missing gear shift that's been stuck in hover mode since 1983. I've never forgiven that kid. And I probably never will.

Discovering My Joystick

But as much as I loved Star Wars, I loved video games more. Which is why, on one sorry day in 1982 when I was home from school due to a lucky outbreak of chicken pox, I was so excited when my dad

brought home an Atari 2600 from the electronics store. He'd rented it for me since I didn't have much else to do with my time other than scratch in places I shouldn't, so I took to it instantly.

He didn't bring home much in the way of games, though. In fact, the only cartridge he rented along with the system was some sort of typical blast-the-bad-guys-from-the-bottom-of-the-screen type of affair, but I loved it all the same. I played the heck out of that game, so much so that when it came time to return the beautiful wood-grained monster, my dad just bought it from the store. And there it stayed in our house for the next many years, tucked away in what we called The TV Room.

Not long after I'd recovered from chicken pox, my sister and I came down with Mononucleosis. Given its common name of "The Kissing Disease" this was unfortunate for many reasons, and did nothing to help my confusion over that scene in Empire when Luke does a little tongue wrestling with Leia because Obi-Wan was a little too slow figuring out that it might be a good idea to let the kid know the princess is his sister before the two start getting the hots for each other. But yeah, I didn't get it from my sister. Or maybe I did and I've blocked it out. Either way, let's move on.

I had a cousin who was working for Motorola around that time, and it turned out that his company was one of the primary chip manufacturers for Atari cartridges. This meant that he had access to virtually every game that came down the pipeline, including some that never made it to market. All it took to play them was an open cartridge with a ZIF socket, and you could swap out one chip for another and play every game you ever wanted. And I did, just as soon as he brought me several stacks of black foam with chips stuck in them. I went from having three, maybe four games to hundreds. And I became very, very popular at school.

At first, no one believed that I had so many games. My parents weren't rich or divorced and showering me with gifts to buy my greedy love or anything, so there was no logical reason why I should be so lucky as to have hundreds of Atari games. (I don't remember the actual count, but it was anywhere from 150-250, including dozens of unreleased ROMs - all of which I lost in one of the many hurricanes that hit my area over the years. If I still had them today, I could probably sell them and retire to some tropical paradise somewhere even though I don't really like the tropics. Still, it's what you do.)

It took the testimony of a few friends who'd witnessed the glory of my stacks of chips to win the confidence of my second grade classmates, but after that, everyone wanted to come to my birthday parties. So it kinda sucked when the whole thing came to a screeching halt after the big video game crash of '83 and no one wanted to play with me anymore.

Which led to one of the best things that ever happened to me: the Apple][.

Or at least a pretty awesome clone.

Chapter Two

Christmas, 1983

In the months and weeks leading up to every Christmas morning of my childhood, my parents, being a strange and conniving pair of offspring generators, would begin the annual tradition of convincing me and my sister that we lived in a Dickensian tragedy of abject poverty. We were told to expect no presents each year, on account of how we were likely to be shipped off to a workhouse at any given moment.

While the presents under the tree from my parents were usually pretty thin on account of the aforementioned lack of money, Santa always came through. I don't know how he did it, or why (I was a pretty obnoxious kid, so I'm not sure how my name ever left the Naughty list), but every Christmas morning, there would be a bunch of new presents under the tree, all from good St. Nick. There were always a lot of smaller presents, things I asked for and some things I didn't even know I wanted, and there was usually one big present, which was always the one thing I never expected to get, but somehow always did.

One year, it was a bicycle: a Team Murray dirt bike, with a royal blue paint job, garish yellow pads, and a black plastic torture-seat that hurt in all the wrong places.

Another year, it was my first Nintendo, which also happened to be *the* first Nintendo because this was  the '80s and the NES had just come out. But this was the year I got my very first computer, which was also one of the very first computers because, again, this was the '80s and no one had come up with smartphones and iPads yet.

My dad was working in the repair department of an electronics store at the time, which meant he was always bringing home interesting gizmos. As I've already mentioned, once when I had chicken pox and had to stay home from school for a week, he checked an Atari 2600 out from the store and brought it home for me to play instead of going to class and doing homework like the suckers who didn't have the foresight to come down with an infectious disease. He never brought home a computer though, because nobody considered computers to be consumer electronics yet, so the store didn't have any. Computers were meant for big business and dorky kids, while electronics stores were the exclusive domains of stereos, televisions, and the almighty VCR.

Still, my dad having access to so many electronic gizmos had its downsides, like when my mother began Christmas morning in 1983 by saying, "Wait in the hall with your sister until Dad finishes setting up the video camera."

His unlimited access to gadgetry was beginning to take its toll.

This was back before you could just whip out your iPhone to record a video. Instead, there was a lengthy setup period involving plugging a giant, over-the-shoulder camera into an actual VCR you had strapped under one arm while the other began the bizarre finger waggling necessary to sync the camera to the recorder and set the white balance and fiddle with all the other arcane mysteries of 1980s video technology. Of course, this was only after you'd already rigged up enough lights to trigger a full-scale DEA assault today, just so you could kinda-sorta make out the various quivering shapes as human when you played the tape back later.

The downside to all of this video prep work to an overexcited kid waiting to see what Santa Claus brought him was that I was stuck in the hallway for what seemed like just shy of ten minutes past eternity. The upside, of course, was that the video couldn't instantly be uploaded to the Internet, because Al Gore hadn't invented it yet.

"Okay, come in!" my mother shouted in the hesitant tone of someone who doesn't know if the red light on the camera means it is - or isn't - working.

A half-second later...

"No, wait! Stay there!" she yelled, panicked. My sister and I could make out the muffled voice of my dad trying to convince her that everything was fine. "Are you sure?" we heard her ask, worry and disbelief dripping from her question mark.

"Yes, sugar. The red light means it's on," replied my dad in the slightly increased volume and annoyed tone of someone who's just realized that conspiratorial whispering isn't going to cut it.

"But is it recording?"

"Yes, honey."

"Are you sure? Because the VCR doesn't look like it's recording."

"Is the red light on?"

"Yes."

"Then it's recording."

"Okay. But are you sure?"

My father's sigh was audible far in the hallway as my sister and I finally decided to just sit down, leaning against the stuccoed wall while we waited. After about five more minutes of persuasion followed by confusion, followed by frustration, followed by reluctant acceptance, we finally got the all clear to come into the living room.

Approximately .0003 seconds later, I lost my dang mind.

Insanity, it should be noted before we go any further, is a legal term rather than a clinical one. It is sometimes used in courtrooms to defend the crazy actions of crazy people, on account of how they can't be held responsible for all the crazy stuff they've done because they're just so filled with crazy. However, it is primarily used to defend the crazy actions of sane people who, for whatever reason, briefly come completely unhinged and run around, doing stupid things. This is called Temporary Insanity, and the point is that it has absolutely no bearing on whether a person is actually crazy or not. It's just one of those things that happens inexplicably, like Austria's Falco. Or blue eye shadow.

"WHAAAAAAAT?!?!?!?!" I screamed as I rounded the corner and saw the gorgeous yellowed box of computational glory that would take over my life for the next few years. It was already plugged in and turned on, with a small television set on top of the case as a monitor. Again, I screamed. "A COMPUUUUTERRRRR?!"

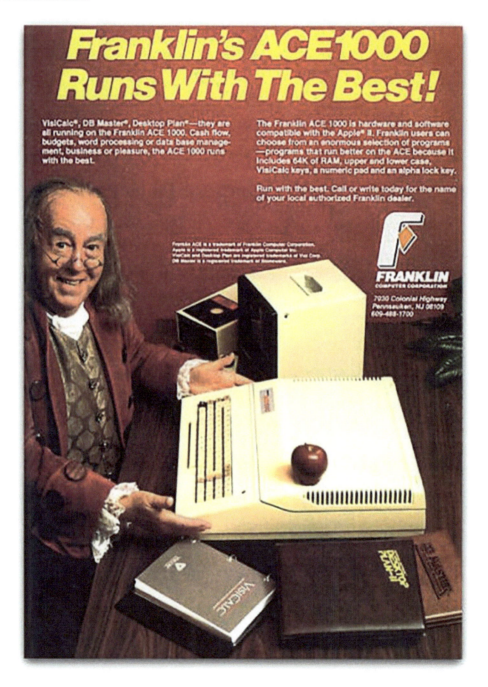

I spent the next few minutes chanting some variation of the words what and computer while flailing my body around in the most spastic way imaginable. (This is saying something if you can imagine me as a skinny little kid with a bowl cut and freakishly long arms. I was basically one of those things you see outside used car lots that flap around in the wind and gyrate uncontrollably about low, low prices.)

At some point, I calmed down and stopped embarrassing myself, but the videographic evidence remains to this day. Fortunately, it's currently trapped between dimensions in the magnetic tape of a VHS cassette, and I have no plans of releasing it into the world. So don't ask.

I have no real memory of anything else I got that Christmas. When I look back on that morning, all I can really see is the title screen to a game called In Search Of The Most Amazing Thing flashing on the television monitor of my Franklin Ace 1000. The computer was one of the many Apple][clones that flooded the market in the days before Apple employed specialized assassination squads to murder anyone even thinking about copying their engineering, which meant it was pretty much an exact copy of the famous personal computer that launched personal computing.

And I loved it.

I played with it for the rest of the day, and nearly every day afterward for years. My dad and I bonded over shared gaming experiences, I learned how to type and how to write on it, and I eventually made friends with it once modems came along and I could call other people with my computer and talk to them with my keyboard. But that morning, all I could see was my dreams coming true. Again. And looking back, all I can see today is the same thing. Because, if you can manage to hold onto it, Christmas Magic never leaves you, no matter how old you get.

(There's more to the story of Christmas 1983. A lot more, but since it's not exactly gaming or geek related, you'll need to pick up my other book, *A Lifetime of Questionable Decisions*, to read it. Sorry. I'm the worst.)

Enter the solitude

By the end of the second grade, I was more or less out of the "friends" I'd made during my Atari days. Sure, there were a few kids I knew that still liked to come hang out with me, but they were all infected with a severe case of nerdism, so they didn't count. (Except that they did and I just didn't realize it at the time, on account of how I'd also been infected with the dread disease and just hadn't been smart enough to realize it yet. I would, though. And soon.)

My second-grade class was called "The Apple Core" because our teacher had a thing for apples, both the fruit and the computers. Our classroom was completely decked out with both.

A typical day in the Apple Core often meant arriving early and staying late, although this was more of a problem specific to my own experience rather than a summary of the average day for the rest of my classmates. At some point during the day, my teacher would say to me, "Go get your Apple, Kristian."

And I'd go get my apple, which was a bit of red construction paper cut out in the shape of the fruit. Every time we did something good in class, the teacher would make us go get our apples so she could whip out a hole-punch and stab a tiny circle or two into the paper. She called these "nibbles" and they were the currency of the classroom. If you wanted to use the bathroom, you needed nibbles. If you wanted to go to recess, you traded nibbles for time. And, if you were like me and the only thing you cared about was getting to use the computer, you needed nibbles for that, too. So I loved bringing her my apple.

Of course, the teacher hadn't quite worked out all the kinks in her system. For one, any fool with a hole-punch could create their own nibbles, which was surprisingly easy to get away with, provided you didn't get too greedy with it. Second, since her currency was subtractive rather than additive as concerns the paper of the apples, it was impossible for her to remove nibbles once they'd been spent. If you were bad in class, she'd just rip your apple in half and toss it in the trash - but if you hadn't done anything wrong, you got to keep your apple if you had a remainder of nibbles after concluding whatever trades you'd made with her.

The smart kids (us nerds) figured out early on to always leave a few nibbles on the apple, rather than use them all up in one go. That way, she'd put your apple back on the paper tree she'd constructed on one of the room's cork boards. And, the frantic life of a second-grade teacher being what it is, she would promptly forget that you'd used any of your nibbles. Between sneaking a hole-punch into class and our teacher's lack of foresight concerning the remainder situation, my friends and I got a lot of computer time. All two of us.

We'd often stay in at recess to get some computer time in so we could die of dysentery or infect our wagon trains with cholera. And when our parents were late picking us up, we'd while away the time selling digital lemonade...when I wasn't busy cleaning out my desk, of course.

Our teacher had a habit of periodically dragging my desk into the middle of the classroom at the end of the day and dumping its contents onto the floor. I was a bit of a hoarder in those days (and my wife will say I still am), so this was her way of making me purge: through public humiliation and staying after school.

But I like to think she was just looking for the hole-punch.

Searching for the most amazing thing

I spent the better part of the year at home with my Franklin, trying to complete the game I'd gotten for Christmas. It was a fun, if infuriating, little game from Spinnaker Software. Technically, it was *edutainment*, but this was over a decade before some jerk invented the term during the '90s dot com boom. To me, it was just a game, much like Oregon Trail, Lemonade Stand, or the truck driving sim we played at school where you lived the glorious, text-based life of a long-haul trucker. Yeah, we were easily amused in the '80s.

Anyway, In Search of the Most Amazing Thing started off with you, the player, being summoned by your Uncle Smoke Bailey to go searching for *the most amazing thing*. He provided you a ship called the B-Liner, which let you explore the world and interact with its shy inhabitants, who you communicated with by way of drawing out little line patterns that the game turned into tones called Musix. It was a weird little game.

I spent hours, days, weeks and months subsisting on the questionably-named food called Popberries while dodging deadly Mire Crabs in my jetpack and gathering intel from Musix trades, all with the singular purpose of discovering what (and where) the most amazing thing was. Unfortunately, I had no idea what I was doing.

The universe of In Search Of was divided into the surface world and the underworld of the Mire. The game constantly warned you against going into the Mire, and suggested you get out as quickly as possible if you ever went spelunking beneath the surface. It was so dead-set against you strapping on your jetpack to go underground (yeah, it didn't make a lot of sense) that it was pretty much the last thing you'd ever do.

So naturally, it's exactly what I did.

One day, after finally getting so frustrated with the game that I decided to just murder my little pixelated character before rage quitting the game forever, I took him deep into the Mire. Very deep. So deep, in fact, that I eventually got bored and just wedged a book onto the joystick so he'd keep flying to the bottom of the Mire, sinking further and further into inky blackness with each refresh of the screen. So gleeful was I during these final moments of the little jerk's life that I actually remember sitting there, watching him fall while I stared at the screen and smiled. The dude was going to die, and I was going to watch it happen. Evil had taken hold.

Except the guy never died. He just kept on falling and falling and falling. I was beginning to lose patience and was about to just switch off the computer and do something sensible like give the floppy disk a nice warm bath in soothing lighter fluid when it happened. The screen dissolved into nothingness and a bit of text began typing itself before my very eyes. I don't remember the exact wording, but it was something along the lines of, "Congratulations, kiddo. You found it! The Most Amazing Thing is...YOU!"

I just sat there, blinking my eyes in disbelief. After months of struggling to complete this game, I'd finally done it. On accident. While trying to murder the main character.

To this day, I don't know if I just got lucky and accidentally exploited a bug in the game's code, or if the programmer actually meant to bury the end of the game at the bottom of the Mire for whoever eventually discovered it through research and determination. In my case, it was pure homicidal rage. All I knew was that I'd finally won, and I was done with the game. I felt great about that.

And a little ripped off. It was kind of a lame ending. Besides, I already knew I was amazing. Spinnaker Software could have saved us both a lot of time by just admitting that up front.

In any event, as soon as I walked away from the computer, I immediately called all one of my friends to tell him the news...and I distinctly remember how excited he wasn't. He didn't seem to be impressed at all, which served as my first lesson in the harsh realities of life: No one cares about your nonsense achievements but you.

Unfortunately, that particular lesson is one that would haunt me for the rest of my life, straight through to the present day.

Chapter Three

I played a lot of games on my Apple][clone. A lot of games. But only a handful managed to wedge themselves firmly between the squishy folds of my memory so tightly that they're inseparable from my thoughts of childhood. There was In Search of the Most Amazing Thing (which I've already talked about, in case you're skipping around chapters like some kind of monster) and there was Rescue Raiders, which was a favorite of my dad's, much to my horror. He was always stealing the computer to play it. An unforgivable crime.

He would do things like insist that I do my homework immediately after dinner under the pretense that it would probably build character or whatever, but I knew his real agenda was just to squeeze in some time in the chopper before I could get to the computer.

And if he was in the middle of a particularly tense battle, I could just forget about claiming my birthright whenever I got finished with the reading and the writing and the arithmeticking. He'd sit there

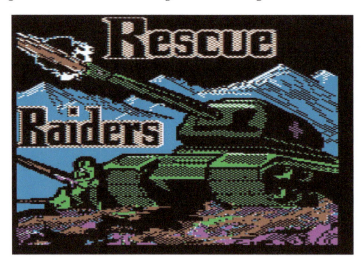

for however long it would take him to either save the day or go down in flames - sometimes for what seemed like hours - all the while making this obnoxious little sucking sound with his teeth each time he pressed the fire button. Each and every time.

Seriously, it wasn't right. It was both a sucking and a hissing sound at the same time, as if he was both inhaling and exhaling simultaneously with a blatant disregard for the laws of human physiology. And it was super annoying.

But computer time wasn't always competitive. Not when Ultima was involved.

Ultima II was my first Real Computer Game, and my first exposure to the roleplaying genre. I loved it immediately.

The brainchild of famed game designer, private astronaut, rabid collector, and all around groovy dude, Richard Garriott, the Ultima series literally consumed my childhood. Starting with picking up a copy of Ultima II at Software Rental (the cleverly named store that rented software for the five minutes or so back in the '80s when you could actually rent software) and ending with never (because I still go back and play through some of the games every now and then, to this day), Ultima came to define much of what I remember about growing up geek.

It had dungeons and it had dragons and, in the case of the early Ultimas, it had spaceships and time travel and ultimate evil overlords that you could only defeat with the aggressive use of punch cards. (Seriously. Don't ask.) It had magic and wonder, and over the course of the series, it became its own world. My world. Mine and my dad's.

Suffering a bit of downsizing around the time Ultima II came out, my dad suddenly served a brief stint as Mr. Mom for a period. During this time, my mom went back to teaching, while my dad stayed at home and took care of the housework and the picking up of the kids from school, and that sort of thing. And ordering a whole lot of junk with UPC symbols and coupons clipped from god knows where, but we ended up with a cool porcelain Pillsbury DoughBoy cookie jar and some sweet Kool-Aid plastic dinnerware. Or maybe it was just a pitcher shaped like the Kool-Aid Man and some cups. It's all a bit hazy.

Anyway, one Friday we went and rented Ultima II along with a nifty little program called Copy][Plus that let you copy most any game the store had in stock. It cost more to rent, of course, but since you could use Copy][Plus to copy Copy][Plus and then use it again whenever you wanted, it was a

good investment. So we copied Ultima II (and later III and IV, but not V because it needed, like, 64 whole Ks of RAM, and I only had a measly 48), then set about on our quest to save the world.

Of course, when I say we copied Ultima II, I mean that we *technically* copied it because there were issues. I don't know what kind of copy protection the game used, but roughly half the time we tried to boot the game, the disc drive would just sit there yelling at us with grindy noises while its red light blinked disapprovingly.

Convinced that the game somehow *knew* we'd broken the law and copied it, I eventually decided that, if it didn't see me, it wouldn't get mad at me and would boot up properly. So I would hide under the desk every single time I tried to boot the game, while spying on the monitor from its reflection in a mirror that was hanging on my closet door. I was a simple child.

(And yes, we ending up pirating three of the first four Ultima games. But Lord British officially pardoned me a little while back, so everything's fine now. Don't call the cops.)

Every Ultima came with a cloth map, which I credit (and my wife blames) for my adult obsession with cartography. I use maps as decoration, hanging them up on our walls like fine art from Middle Earth and Britannia, and other realms far beyond the distant unknown. Ultima 2 took place on Earth, however. (Others took place in Britannia. My second home.)

My dad and I invented co-op gaming before there was co-op gaming, by way of sharing a save file between us. The deal worked like this: Dad would play in-between doing the dishes or watching his stories or whatever the hell else he did while I was at school, and I'd play in the evenings after I finished my homework. We'd fill each other in on what we did and what we discovered at the end of each shift, and we worked our way through the game one little bit at a time.

Eventually, it became a race to see who would be the one playing when we completed the game. (Spoiler alert: it was me.)

One random morning when I'd woken up and gotten myself ready uncharacteristically early, I sat down to squeeze in a little play time and try once again to defeat the evil sorceress Minax, whose castle we'd made it to, but who neither one of us had yet figured out how to defeat. Until that morning.

It was tense, but I figured out whatever puzzle it was that had us stuck. I think it involved needing a ring or some such to pass through some forcefields or whatnot, and I'd put it on and away we went. But the crafty witch just kept teleporting all over the place every time I'd hit her, so the final battle was a long and tedious affair of running all over creation to slap her around a little bit until she eventually croaked.

It ran long, and I got a free tardy note from my dad for being late to school due to a video game. Because some things are important. (It wasn't my first free tardy note, though, or my last. I regularly got them whenever the space shuttle launched during school hours because I was a huge nerd and just had to watch it go up each and every time I could. The first time I didn't, the Challenger exploded. I was in Earth Science class when the announcement came over the PA system and I did my best to sit in class and not break down crying.)

My dad and I kept on playing games together through the years. We played Ultima III and defeated the evil giant robot demon with the aforementioned punch cards. We played Ultima IV, and became virtuous avatars of enlightenment. Then we played Ultima V and it crashed after the intro because I guess the universe has always hated me.

We'd eventually get around to playing again with Ultima VI, but that's a story for later, since it involves my first IBM-compatible PC and a whole new era of my life. You'll just have to wait on that, because between Ultima IV and Ultima VI, a little thing called the BBS happened.

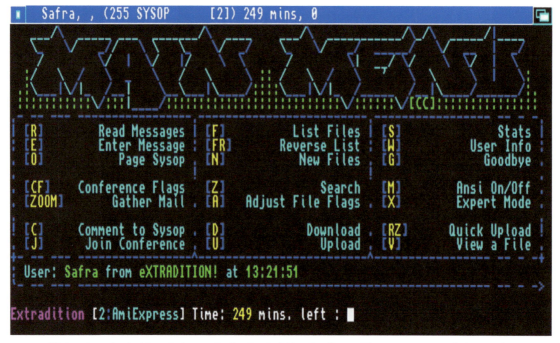

This is what the internet looked like before there was an internet.

Interlude:
Baldur's Gate

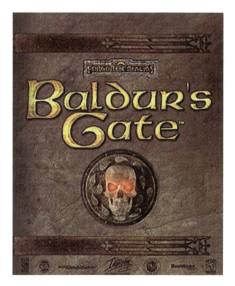

I know Baldur's Gate didn't come out until 1998, which means this feature should technically be in the next Life Bytes book, but I did another one of these for its sequel and I don't want to put two of them in the same book. However, I don't want to deprive you of enjoying my hilarious suffering either, so I jumped forward in time and brought this back from the future. You're welcome.

Before we jump down the BBS rabbit hole, I thought it'd be fun to pause for a minute and interrupt things with this hysterical nightmare of a story. Way back when Baldur's Gate was being heralded as the great savior bringing the CRPG back from the brink of death, I hated it. I've always hated it.

Maybe it was all the numbers. I don't like math in my roleplaying. Maybe it was the crazy D&D rules. I don't know. I just know that I never cared for it, no matter how many times I tried to get into it. But this time, I was prepared to go the distance by playing the full game to see if it changed my mind.

First, let's just get the 800-pound dragon out of the way up front: Advanced Dungeons and Dragons. I hate it. But I also love it. But I hate it, too. I've always loved D&D, ever since I got my first red box starter kit. I created tons of characters with detailed backstories, complex relationships, and interesting motivations. I designed intricate campaigns with branching plotlines and living NPCs. And then I didn't do anything with any of it.

I never actually played D&D, because I didn't have anyone to play D&D with. I was a weird kid, a huge nerd, and hopelessly socially awkward. Sure, I had a few friends, but any of them who might've actually played D&D had religious parents of the sort that thought rolling dice is the first step on the road to Hell. (This being during the Satanic Panic years of the '80s coupled with living in the Deep South, parental prohibition of RPGs was a pretty common childhood trauma.)

In short, I never really got to play with the AD&D rules apart from pretending to play the game in my head whenever I'd crack out my rulebook and work on a new character. And Baldur's Gate is nothing if not slavishly devoted to the AD&D rules. Which are kinda stupid.

Honestly, some of them just make no sense at all. Sure, they're logical from a mechanical perspective, but the fiction wrapped around some of the game systems just makes no sense at all. Take mages, for instance. They have to memorize spells every night, then go to sleep to fully commit them to memory (for some reason) before they can be cast. This makes sense from a gameplay perspective, as it adds an element of pre-planning to encounters. But on the other hand, it's completely bonkers.

Imagine being a mage in the D&D universe. You work hard and master a new spell, memorize how to cast it and then excitedly fall asleep, eager to wake up the next morning and cast Magic Missile at the pre-dawn darkness or whatever. So you do that. AND IT IS AMAZING.

Then what? You're standing there, all zippy-zap happy with yourself, AND YOU HAVE NO IDEA HOW YOU DID WHAT YOU JUST DID. Because you forgot the instant you cast the spell.

Imagine this same logic applying to anything else in the D&D universe. Learn to tie your shoes? Great job! Just pray they don't come untied during the day, because you're not going to remember how to do that neat bunny rabbit trick until you teach yourself anew and fall asleep all over again. Learn a new sword technique? Awesome! You use it to kill an orc that was attacking you, but now you're just standing there, clueless and clutching your sword, wondering where the pointy end goes. You'll need to learn how to fight again before bedtime. Meanwhile, you were just murdered by an angry rabbit. Sorry.

D&D mages are all madmen. They have to be. Every moment of their lives dangles upon a precipice between absolute power and complete imbecility. Sisyphus had it easier.

But anyway, back to Baldur's Gate. A few years ago, I was determined to figure out what people love about this game - and boy, people do love it - so I committed to doing a full playthrough. Again. Only this time, I'd finish the dang thing and document my entire experience. It turned out pretty great.

It begins.

Part One

SHUT UP, IMOEN!

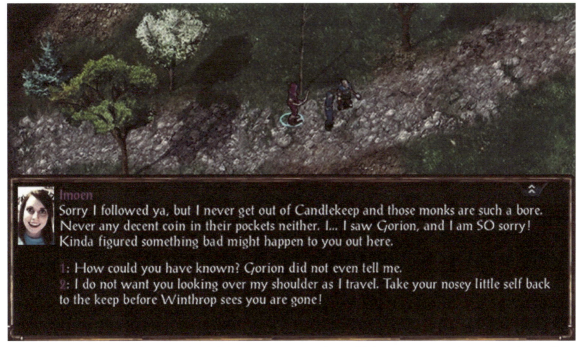

Imoen

Sorry I followed ya, but I never get out of Candlekeep and those monks are such a bore. Never any decent coin in their pockets neither. I... I saw Gorion, and I am SO sorry! Kinda figured something bad might happen to you out here.

1: How could you have known? Gorion did not even tell me.
2: I do not want you looking over my shoulder as I travel. Take your nosey little self back to the keep before Winthrop sees you are gone!

At least you can change the character portraits. This one seemed appropriate for Imoen, with apologies to Laina Morris.

Oh, god. I forgot about this useless mess of pixels called a companion. Her name is Imoen, and her voice is the best example of why having limited voice acting in these games is a blessing. Although ostensibly a thief of some repute, she is basically useless in all things that don't involve annoying the ever loving snot out of me every five seconds.

She's also the first companion you get, once you finally make it out of the tutorial town with all of its creepy green-robed monks groping at your tender bits under the guise of "helping" you. Yeah, I know what you're about, Mister Creeper-Robe. We all know.

Anyway, once you leave the safety of Candlekeep, your foster father or stepdad or cradle-robing sketchy uncle spirits you away under cover of darkness. And is immediately blown up.

You get ambushed, and he tells you to RUN! So your character slowly - and good lord, do the characters in this game putter about with all the speed of tranquilized sloths - meanders off the screen while a whole bunch of fizzledly-plop happens with magic and particle effects until your great-grand-dad or wise old mentor or whatever the hell he was finally blows up and dies, not necessarily in that order.

After that, you wake up the next morning and butter my biscuits, if it isn't Imoen coming merrily down the way, cheerfully proclaiming that you're a queer fellow before acknowledging that, yeah, she knows the guy who raised you as his own child was just brutally exploded before your very eyes the night before. But hey, she really wanted to get out of Candlekeep and see the world, so heya! She's coming with you, whether you like it or not.

So, fine. Come on, maybe you'll die soon. I don't really care.

We quickly come across a couple of shady dudes named Xzar and Montaron, because you always meet people with high scoring Scrabble names like Xzar in these sorts of games. They both seem intractably evil, and Xzar is obviously insane, but who the hell cares? I need meat shields. Join up!

They want to explore some mine or something, but I'm supposed to go to the Friendly Arms Inn and meet someone named Khalid or something. According to my uncle grandpa or whatever he was, Khalid will help me in my quest. I don't doubt this, because there was a guy named Khalil who owned a convenience store near my house when I was in high school, and he never checked IDs. I figure they're probably related, so I've already got an opener.

Unfortunately, before we get there, Imoen runs the hell off to chase butterflies or something because god knows the pathfinding in this game is EXCEPTIONAL, and the next thing I know, she's being attacked by a wolf. So we run over to save her sorry butt, and Montaron bites the big one. Sorry to see you go, weird little dude. But them's the breaks.

I mourn his passing by taking all his gear, then we head out on our way. Finally, we arrive at the Inn and we're immediately attacked. Xzar gets blown up, but we kill the bad guy.

I loot both their corpses, then take a pee on Xzar's cold body because he quoted Hannibal Lector earlier for some reason, which just kind of pissed me off because this is supposed to be the one damn fantasy world where Anthony Hopkins doesn't exist.

Anyway, it's just me and freaking Imoen again because she just refuses to die, so we head into the Inn to meet Khalid. Hopefully, he'll kill her for me...

Hooray! Half of us made it.

Part Two
DAMMIT, IMOEN!

I meet Khalid in a corner of the inn. He st-st-stutters, either from an unfortunate speech impediment that I would never make fun of, or because he's a terrified little weasel, crapping himself at shadows. It could go either way, really.

He introduces me to someone named Jaheira, who talks with that perfect THIS SOUNDS FOREIGN accent used by C-list actors everywhere, and tells me that they need to go to the same damn place the other guys I picked up needed to go to.

Everybody wants to go to the Nashkel Mines, I guess. Which is kind of like Nashville, but with less banjo and more medieval stuff or something. Whatever. I just don't care anymore.

Jaheira tells me, "We'll leave as soon as you're ready, though it should be soon." Which I take to mean, "Take your time as long as we leave right the hell now, idiot man-child. "So we leave.

Or try to, at least. As soon as we hit the door, a disembodied voice scolds me from the beyond. "You must gather your party before venturing forth," it commands.

SON OF A… Where the hell is Imoen?!

I find Imoen continuously walking back and forth between a very fat man and a very inanimate chair. Clearly, she was stymied by their lack of movement. Mother frakkin' Imoen…

I take the shoe-licker by her hand and lead her to the door, and now we leave. But not before I notice that I'm apparently carrying around two corpses with me.

The dead guys we picked up along the way are still dead, and their portraits are blanked out on my screen. Why? I don't know. Because the game doesn't tell you squat. It's like that. Instead, it wants you to CONSULT THE MANUAL.

Which, it must be said, was pretty common for games back in the olden times. However, whereas most manuals often included as much flavor text and lore as they did instructions, Baldur's Gate wasn't about to hear any of that world-building noise, and instead hits you with a GIANT TOME OF ARCANE MATH. 125 pages of it, to be exact. And don't even think about skipping it, or you'll be lugging around corpses with no clue what to do with them other than continue apologizing to everyone you meet for the smell.

It turns out, I can resurrect the poor bastards at a temple. Great! There was a temple back in Candlekeep, where I grew up. We'll just fast travel back there, bring these decomposing wretches back to life, and head on to fortune and glory in the mines.

TO CANDLEKEEP!

Except of course it couldn't be that easy. We trek back to the place I just left not two days ago, which takes TWENTY HOURS of game time to get back to, and I strut up to the door. I say howdy do to the friendly guard at the door, who then tells me to piss off and I can't come in.

Why not? Because suddenly those little green creeper-robe monks need A SPECIAL BOOK THAT I DON'T KNOW WHAT IT IS before they'll let me back in gates of the town I spent my entire life in, minus the past couple of days when I was out saving the world and watching my stepdad foster uncle whatever be blown into tiny fleshchunks right in front of me. You'd think that'd get them to cut me a little slack, right? WRONG.

Fine. BACK TO NASHKEL!

KEEPER OF THE PORTAL: I am sorry, friend. I know that you are the child of Gorion and have dwelt here all your life, but I cannot exempt anyone from the sanctions of the most high Ulraunt.

JELT: Egh... how tedious all this becomes.

"Egh...how tedious all this becomes."13

We walk all the way back to Nashkel, Tennessee, where I wander around, looking for a temple. Along the way, I meet up with some kind of untamed witch or something who has a voice almost as annoying as Imoen's. She tells me that some bandits are after her, so I help out and murder them by clicking I don't know what until they're all dead. Then, she joins my party and I walk into the Inn to rest from my wounds, where I am subsequently MURDERED IN THE PANCREAS BY AN ASSASSIN.

MOTHER DAMMIT, THIS GAME.

I load my quicksave and try again. And again. And again. I eventually kill the amazing murderbot sent to destroy me, but not before she KILLS EVERYONE IN MY PARTY except myself...and Imoen. Of course.

"Heya! You're a queer fellow!"

ARGH! Fine, Imoen. Just...fine. Let's go find the stupid temple.

We find the stupid temple, which happily resurrects my fallen comrades for a paltry 100 gold pieces per useless fathead, which is up from two useless fatheads at this point, to four useless fatheads. Not counting Imoen, of course, who remains a useless fathead, but who stubbornly refuses to die.

So we're all resurrected, and we go back and rest at the Inn, which is now blissfully free of assassin murder droid wizard thingies. A good night's rest later, and it's finally off to the mines...

We make to it to mines without much incident, although I slay enough Gibberlings - whatever the hell those are - until I just stop feeling. Anything.

I meet some dude named Something Stupid That I Don't Remember, and he tells me something like, "Oh, wailey wailey! The mines is overrun and the iron has all gone bad and save us, won'tcha please and thank you kindly!" Only he gives me just one day to do it, (but the joke's on him because I end up sleeping at least three weeks inside those damn mine shafts while I heal between every incessant battle with ridiculous kobold maniacs).

We enter the mines. We kill things. Lots of things. I feel nothing. I eventually even stop looting the corpses of my fallen enemies because I've lost the will to care anymore. Plus, it's an enormous pain in the ass and I keep running out of inventory slots, and what the hell does any of it matter, anyway? I mean, what's the point of it all, when you get right down to it?

Hope is a fragile tinderbox.

We are lost.

blink

Um, sorry. Kind of zoned out for a second there. I'm back. Where were we, again? Oh, yes. The mines. We're fighting kobolds and killing kobolds and ignoring the bodies of kobolds while working our way ever deeper and deeper into the labyrinthine depths of Tennessee's forgotten iron mines. Until...we aren't anymore.

We go down what appears to be yet another shaft and suddenly emerge into daylight. This can't be right, though, because we haven't cleared the mines or whatever the hell we were supposed to do yet, so we have to go back in.   Only we can't go back in.

BECAUSE OF COURSE WE CAN'T GO BACK IN.

The exit apparently crumbled behind us and there's no way back in from this side. We'll have to go all the way back around to the main entrance, then make our way down the **entire mine system** again.

It was at this point that I felt myself beginning to lose the will to live...

Fast travel back to Nashville. Zoom down to the mine entrance. Go inside. Murder more kobolds. Descend. Murder even more kobolds. Descend. Keep murdering kobolds. Descend. Aaaaaaaand...here we are, right back where we were before we left out of the exit that didn't look anything like an exit.

I start sliding my cursor around the screen, looking for something - anything - I might have missed. And I find it. Apparently, there's a "cave" inside the mines, which I thought were already kind of a cave but you know what? Screw it. Whatever, I don't even care anymore. Onward!

I walk into the cave, kill some more kobolds, then meet a funky wizard named Xan who asks if he can join my party. Sure, pal. Why not? The more the merrier!

But my party is full. He can't join unless I leave someone behind. Oh, what to do? What to do? GOODBYE, IMOEN!

Xan joins up, and I move to another room within the cave, where there's a bad dude named Mulahey who's behind the whole tainted ore business with the kobolds or something. They've been dripping some sort of vial on the iron that makes it go bad or I don't even freaking know. Or care. I ATTACK.

It's at this point that I suddenly discover that I've recruited yet another useless fathead into my party. Xan has apparently memorized exactly zero spells the whole time he's been sitting alone in this cave with literally nothing else to do other than memorize his dang spells. SO HE DIES.

Fortunately, so does Mahoney or whatever his name was, and now I can finally end the quest and reveal the truth except my inventory is full again and this guy was carrying a ton of crap that I have to lug back and where did my life go so very, very wrong?

So I make with the round robin of inventory distribution until I've picked his bloated corpse clean, and we go back out the exit that supposedly was rendered impassable when we passed through it earlier, but which is now totally fine for whatever holy hell reason, and we leave. But not before picking up Imoen. **Again.**

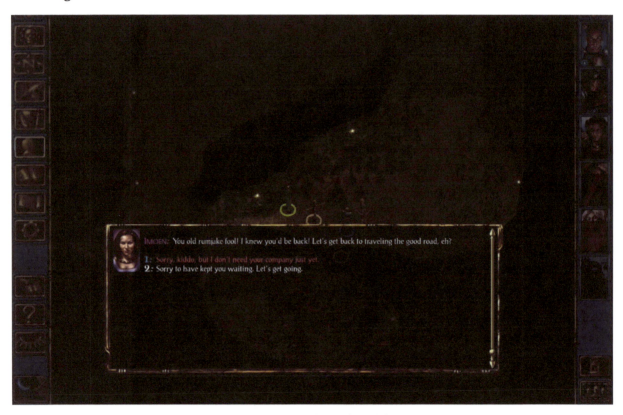

My nerves can't take this.

We head back to Narwhal and I go up to the mayor to tell him the good news. Except it wasn't the mayor because who the heck can tell people apart in this lunatic world of endless pixel clone people. Instead, it was a dude named Minsc.

He wanted to know if he and his hamster could join my party and sure, you've got a miniaturized giant space hamster or whatever, but adding you means I can kick Imoen to the curb again, so you're a beautiful bald bastard and I love you.

GOODBYE, IMOEN!

Part Three
GO FOR THE EYES, BOO!

I pick up Minsc and start looking for the mayor again. I wander over near the inn where I was attacked by the murderbot assassin earlier, and I'm attacked. Again. Neera, my untamed wild mage, dies in the fight, but then a monk appears and asks me if I have a moment to talk about his lord and savior. I don't really pay much attention, but then he asks if he can join my party. He's a monk in Dungeon and Dragons, which means he's probably the Forgotten Realms equivalent of Kung Fu mastery is, so I take him on.

We get waylaid a lot.

But now my party is full and I have to let someone go. Since Jaheira basically just entangles the entire party in her magical Entangle vines every single time she's cast the stupid spell, I show her the door.

She openly questions my wisdom, then stomps off in a huff, taking Khalid with her. Apparently, they're a package deal. Explains the stuttering, at least.

I head inside the inn to rest and start identifying all the different magical items I've picked up. This involves a lengthy cycle of having my crazy, Hannibal and Oppenheimer quoting madman of a mage memorize two Identify spells a day, then sleeping all night so he can cast them in the morning. And then memorize them again, then sleep all night again, then cast them again, then repeat until I'm a hollow shell of my former self.

Eventually, we identify everything (only 1/10th of which are actually useful items) and head over to a merchant to sell all the crap I don't need. I haggle with him and buy some plate mail to protect my sorry butt on the field of battle with these assclowns I call companions watching my back, then we head back outside to try and find the mayor. Again.

After much clicking on and talking to random people, I eventually stumble across him. He thanks me for clearing the mines, pays me some gold and I'm on my way. To find out what way that is, I go to open up my journal, when I suddenly realize that I'm down a party member. With Jaheira having taken her boy toy with her when I kicked her to the curb, I have a vacancy. Which can only mean one thing...

Heya!

NOOOOOOOO!

Sigh. I think I remember Imoen mentioning that she'd wait for me back at the Friendly Arm Inn, so I make the trek back there. Twenty-some-odd hours of in-game walking later, and we arrive. I check the ground floor. She's not there. I check the next floor. Every room. She's not there. I check the third floor and get yelled at by fancy noblepersons aghast that I had the audacity to walk into their rooms after they left their doors wide open. She's not there. Then, it dawns on me. **She stayed in the mines!** I really hate her.

Resigned, I return to the mines. Or try to, anyway. We are waylaid by a pack of wild dogs. We kill them. Then we're waylaid again, this time by a group of thugs led by some dude named Pat Senjak and his totally literate life partner, Vanna White. Except she goes by the name Doratea in D&D, for whatever reason. It's pronounced like tortilla, and now I want tacos. I shouldn't play games on an empty stomach.

Anyway, Senjak tells me I'm going to die if I don't buy a vowel, so I get ready for a fight. Then, his little gang of thieves starts dropping dead for inexplicable reasons when a wild Dorn suddenly appears!

Dorn is a half-orc something or other, who is on a mission of vengeance against Pat and Vanna because I guess he got the one puzzle without an R, S, T, L, N or an E in it and he's never quite moved on, so he starts wailing on them. I join in. We wail until people explode. Good times.

After the fight, Michael Dorn asks if he can join my party. At first, I'm hesitant because I remember what a weakling Worf actually was, but hey, whatever. People can grow. Join up!

Bonus: I have a full party now. Sorry, Imoen!

I go to check my journal when I notice that I leveled up. FINALLY! Let me see what new skills I can get. Oh. Neat. Nothing. Of course. Fine.

My journal says we need to go to a place called Beregost that I passed through earlier, and talk to a guy named Tranzig about something, so we head that way and are waylaid by wolves. We murder them.

Arriving in Beregost, we head to the inn and, for once, we aren't attacked by assassin droids, which is nice. We find Danzig rocking out to some death metal up on the second floor and, yep. I spoke too soon. He attacks me, so I kill him and search his warm corpse. He's carrying a note! It tells me that I should travel to Larswood or Peldvale next, wherever they are. I note that my journal tells me I should travel to this place OR that place, when we both know full well that it really means I'm going to have to go to this place AND that place. Lying piece of crap journal.

Having no idea where these places are, I decide to head back to Nashville and start looking from there, which makes a kind of sense, from a video game logic perspective. Natural progression, sort of thing. We head back and fan out, then stumble upon a carnival. A CARNIVAL!

It's got whimsical tents and everything. Some guy named Zeke barks at me to come rescue a woman who was turned to stone by giving him 500 gold coins. I decline. (So far, it's exactly like an actual carnival.)

(*Sidenote*: I swear I keep hearing the same background laughter sound from Rollercoaster Tycoon. It's eerie.)

I walk into a random tent and a guy tries to pick my pocket by way of announcing it to the entire party. I murder him in the face and take back my money. We head back outside and come across a guy calling himself The Great Gazib and the Amazing Oopah, who is apparently the world's only exploding ogre. I talk to the guy, then an ogre appears and explodes into ogre bits. Neat.

I talk to Gazib again, and Oprah explodes again. Then, he comes back and Gazib runs off and the Queen Of Daytime TV tries to kill me for unclear reasons. We murder her in a violent rage, after which some random performer starts reciting poetry at me like nothing at all just happened.

This is a place of madness.

I look around for the Great Gazib, but can't find him in the sea of pixels that look exactly like the Great Gazib but aren't, and I don't feel like bothering with it. I decided to leave and just go wander the wilderness like a caveman. After a lot of being waylaid by wolves and dogs and bandits, I eventually discover Larswood. (Hetfield Forest, however, remains elusive.)

We take no more than five steps into the woods before Rasaad starts talking about his dumb cult again. He really won't shut up about it, but the dude can explode people with his fists. I consider it a fair trade-off.

We run into a guy named Teven, who demands I surrender my yadda yadda whatever. Rassad hits him with the five-point-palm exploding heart technique. He explodes.

We find Stonehenge and some guy named Osmandi, who thinks I killed his brother and attacks me. I murder him, but he has friends who are cave bears. They kill Dorn, Xzar, and Neera, but Rassad levels up his explode fist. So there's that. Silver lining and all.

A guy named Corsone meanders over, apologizes for Osmandi trying to murder me and all, then tells me about some bandits and leaves. I guess that completes the Larswood portion of my quest. Onward to Peldvale!

I make a quick return trip to Tennessee first though, so I can resurrect my useless companions at the temple. After everyone is alive again, I check the map, and there's a Bandit Camp to the north that I can't fast travel to yet, so I take a gamble and bet that Peldvale is on the way there.

Found Peldvale!

Ignored Peldvale!

We walk straight through this important questing area because screw it, who cares? I just keep shouting, "North, Miss Tessmacher! NORTH!" at my party until they stop asking questions. We go north.

Found the Bandit Camp! We storm the camp, murdering bandits left and right. We push our way into the biggest tent, where we find the bandit leader. We murder the crap out of him.

And he returns the favor.

Everyone dies except for me, Dorn and Rasaad, and I'm barely holding on. I got poisoned somehow, and don't have any antidote potions on me. If I die, it's Game Over because none of my worthless buddies I've been bringing back to life this entire game can be bothered to haul my sorry carcass over to the temple when I bite the big one, but whatever. Screw them.

I just keep sucking back healing potions until I don't die from the poisoning. Eventually, it goes away and I'm all better. I spy a chest in the corner of the tent, so I go open it. AND ALMOST DIE AGAIN.

Turns out, it was trapped. I get zapped with lighting and almost die from static cling, but I find a note in the chest that tells me I need to go to someplace called Cloakwood next, so it's an overall win. It talks about something to do with a hidden base and a competing iron mine. I half expect some Jedi to suddenly come down to settle a trade dispute with Naboo or something equally lame, for all the excitement this plot has going for it so far. But at least there's no Jar-Jar, so there's that. Of course, there's always Imoen...

Never mind.

With most of my party dead, I decide to schlep their useless bodies back to Nashville again, so I can bring them back to life at the temple. Again.

We get there and I pay way too much to resurrect these useless people, and everyone is alive and happy again.

Well, almost everyone. As soon as I RETURN THE GIFT OF LIFE to Minsc, he goes absolutely mental and tries to murder me in the kidneys. It seems he's come back from the dead full of rage because I haven't done whatever the hell it was that he wanted me to do as fast as he wanted me to do it, so he decides that murder is the only option.

Rasaad explodes his pancreas, and Minsc is no longer of this world.

Which means I'm down another party member again.

Dammit, Imoen!

So long, Minsc.

Part Four
The Plot Gets A Slight Coagulant

I start making my reluctant walk of shame all the way back to the Narwhal mines. To find Imoen. Gods help me.

I know I don't need her. I know she's useless and does nothing but annoy me, but I can't abide an empty party slot, and Minsc's sudden and unexpected betrayal has left one open. There's nothing for it. I must find her.

Except she's not there. Anywhere. I search every nook and cranny of those mines; I even go back to the cave within the cave where I thought I'd left her when I picked up whatever useless mage it was whose name I don't remember. But nope. VANISHED.

Then it hits me. I picked her back up after what's-his-name died, and didn't drop her again until I met Minsc. Back in Nashville. DAMMIT, IMOEN!

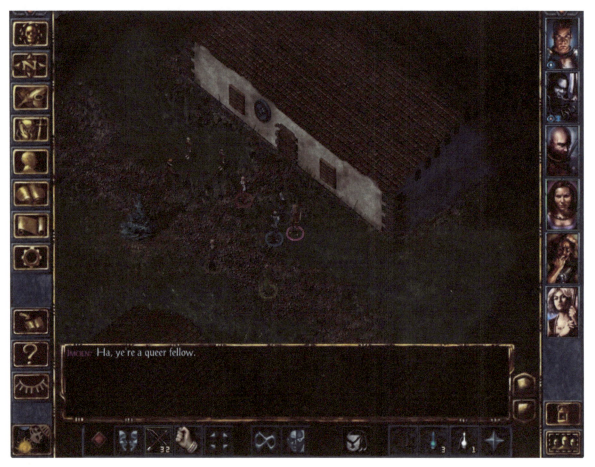

There can be no escape.

I leave the mines and head back to town, where I find the daffy girl still standing there, staring at her shoes. She jumps at the chance to re-join my party for the umpteenth time. I guess she digs me. Whatever.

I check my map, and it looks like I can actually fast travel to Cloakwood Forest, even though I haven't been there yet. Hooray!

I fast travel. I wander around, not noticing that I've already dispelled the entire fog of war for the area; and when I do notice, I chalk it up to maybe one of those notes I read that sent me here had a map scrawled on the back of it or something. I don't question it too much, until I eventually realize that I'm not in Cloakwood at all. I'm in the FIRST DAMN AREA OF THE GAME after the tutorial. You know, where my grandpa uncle stepdad was blown up.

I check my map again and see that Cloakwood is actually farther north. I only thought this was Cloakwood because I guess we didn't have Dora The Explorer when I was growing up, so I never learned how to Map. I mostly just learned how to change my shoes after school for inexplicable reasons thanks to Mister Rogers, and what doing acid probably feels like thanks to The Electric Company.

Anyway, we head north and finally get to Cloakwood. Hooray, progress!

There's a giant house here. Seriously, it's huge. On the outside. But then I go inside and it's like some kind of freaky reverse TARDIS barn because it's absolutely tiny in here. The impossible geometry of this mad world is as inexplicable as it is horrifying. I mustn't dwell too long on it, lest I lose my delicate grasp on what precious little of my sanity remains.

AWAY, INTO THE FOREST!

We step into the next section of Cloakwood Forest and are immediately assaulted by a kid named Tiber, who is all panicked that his brother, Chelak, was named after a resin secreted by the female lac bug because his parents clearly hated him. Also, he took some kind of spider-slaying sword into the woods and hasn't been seen since. Things do not bode well for Shellac, but I promise Tiber that I'll keep my eye out for his desiccated corpse, should I come across it.

We push further into the deep woods, in search of the hidden Iron Throne mine. AND WE FIND IT!

Except we don't, because that would be too easy. Instead, we find a cave that looks a lot like it could've been a mine, if only it had tried harder in school. We walk in and find a morbidly obese, naked spider-man. No, I'm not even kidding.

SO MANY SPIDERS. And Fatty McGee sitting in the middle of the web there was just barking orders the whole time, and I'm not even sure if it was a man and dear god, how does it go to the bathroom and holy hell, does it have a mate? And if so, how do they even...NO. STOP IT.

Some mysteries are best left unanswered.

We kill all the spiders by luring them out of the cave and killing them outside, a few at a time. We do this for two reasons. First, because killing two or three spiders at once is easier than killing a dozen at the same time. Second, because who in the nine Hells could possibly concentrate on fighting when that...thing was undulating all over the place in there. Just. No.

After the spider slayings are done, I go back inside and quickly loot the stash fat boy is sitting next to. Or standing on. Or squatting beside, or lying on top of, or I don't know what. It's impossible to tell. Inside, I find a bunch of loot and, yep. Surprise! The desiccated remains of the unfortunately named Chelak brother. I pick him up because he obviously weighs nothing now that his insides have been liquefied and sucked out, so he fits neatly inside one square of my inventory. Which I guess represents a pocket or something. I have no idea.

So fleshy.

Anyway, we had back to Tiber and break the news to the poor lad. I pull out the dried up husk of a body from my back pocket and ask him if he can identify this pocketful of his brother. He does, then runs off crying. Like he didn't see it coming, the big baby.

He lets me keep the sword though, which comes in handy as I spend the next seventeen years of my life murdering - and being murdered by - giant spiders in the incalculable number of screens that make up Cloakwood Forest.

At some point, I looted the corpse of some creature or another, but ran out of inventory space. I handed a tiny little gem to Imoen so I could pick up a huge sword from the body, and we went on our merry way across the rest of the map. Well, I say we. What I meant was everyone but Imoen.

Giving her that gem was just crossing the damn Rubicon or something with her, because it broke the camel's back AND SHE REFUSED TO MOVE. My entire party walked all the way back over to her to see what her drama queen problem was, and she just stood there like the useless lump of pixels she is.

Apparently, carrying more than a fistful of arrows and an aggressively cheerful attitude is just too much for her delicate flower of a body to handle. She was over-encumbered BECAUSE OF THE GEM THAT DIDN'T WEIGH ANYTHING, so she was just stuck. Completely. Like a turd in a punch bowl.

IMOEN: Encumbered: Cannot move
IMOEN: Encumbered: Cannot move
IMOEN: Encumbered: Cannot move
IMOEN: Encumbered: Cannot move
IMOEN: Encumbered: Cannot move

Do you think she works hard to be this awful, or does it just come naturally?

I took the gem and gave it to someone else who can carry more than half a pound and not die from exhaustion, and she was back to her normal, annoying self. We pushed on.

We killed more spiders and were killed by more spiders. Much quick saving and re-loading were had by all, mostly thanks to all of the traps Imoen set off that she never detected, despite Detecting Traps being the one damn thing she's supposedly good for. We pushed on.

And on.

And on.

Seriously, Cloakwood goes on for days. It stopped feeling like "exploring" about three screens ago, and now it's just Clicking Through Bioware's Cut And Paste Trees for the next few hours. In one section, I meet Eldoth. He looks like kind of a d-bag, but he offers to join my party. I'm not sure he'll be good for anything other than simply Not Being Imoen, so I hire him immediately.

Goodbye, Imoen!

Eldoth tells me about some scheme he has to liberate some gold from somebody I don't give a crap about because I'm not paying attention, and he asks me if I'd be interested in helping him out. I tell him sure, whatever, and we push on.

MOAR CLOAKWOOD!

Wait. I think we found the mines. Finally! We rush in.

Nope. Not a mine. Just a cavern full of murder dragons. Move along, move along.

EVEN MOAR CLOAKWOOD!

Hey, I think we actually found the really real mines this time! I can tell, because the next area that popped up on my map is called Mines. I'm good with context clues.

We rush toward the mines, where we're immediately assaulted by Iron Throne guards. I fight them for a while, but then I accidentally have Xzar cast Horror instead of whatever the hell other button I meant to push, and IT IS AMAZING. All of the bad guys get little shiny disco balls of terror over their heads, and they run around all skibber-skabber instead of trying to poke me with pointy things. It is most excellent.

I meet a guy named Lakadaar next, who asks me what my business is. I tell him that we're here to investigate the evil Iron Throne he works for. He nods and says, "Okey dokey." Then, he tries to kill us all.

Xzar uses Horror. IT'S SUPER EFFECTIVE!

We run into some more guards, but I forgot to rest, so Xzar has forgotten how to cast Horror because I didn't have him memorize it again and he's an idiot. So I click another random spell I haven't bothered with until now, and Neera casts Sleep on a group of thugs.

AND OH MY GOD, it's even better than Horror, because it basically throws The Sandman at bad guys and knocks them right the frak out. Then, they just lie there like little drooling morons (not entirely unlike Imoen) and I get to stab snoring people in their throats until they die. Good times.

ZzzZzzZz. STAB!

We storm the fort and kill a bunch more bad guys while they dream of gumdrops and lollipops, or whatever it is that evil guardsmen dream about. Could be naked fat spider people, for all I know. To each his own.

I run into yet another assassin, who was called Drasus back when he still had a body. But he doesn't anymore because my Kung Fu monk found a magical katana. And that was that.

A guy inside the guard barn tells me that the miners are being held to the east, and asks me not to kill him. I spare his miserable life and head off to save the enslaved miners.

GO EAST.

We go east, to another guardhouse. We head inside, murder some more baddies, then find an elevator in the basement. It takes us down to the mines. At last!

I find myself actually starting to have fun with this game for the first time in ever, which is unsettling. I shake it off and remain focused. I have a job to do. This is no time for feelings.

Once inside the mines, I kill a few guards and talk to some half-naked miners. I don't know why they're half naked or why precious little mining seems to be going on, but I don't ask too many questions. I walk up to one of the freaky freaks who's standing next to a giant circle that looks a lot like a bank vault.

He tells me that it's actually a giant plug stuck into the side of the mines, to keep the river out. Wait. What? There's an actual plug leading to the river? So the mine is underwater, but someone went ahead and left this big hole in it, just in case anyone ever needed to come along and open it to flood the mine? Way to go, Lunatic Mine Architect. Way to go.

Of course, we can't simply pull the plug. It's somehow locked, so I have to find a key first. And maybe try and free all the naked man slaves wandering around the place so they don't get drowned or whatever. I'll see what I can do.

I wander around the mines for a bit, killing the odd guard here and finding the occasional secret door there, until I find another new party member! This guy's a dwarf cleric who goes by the name of Yeslick. Yes, lick. That's his name.

He asks to join up with me, which I'm fine with because he seems a lot more interesting than the ukulele-strumming hipster we picked up earlier. Sorry, Eldoth. Them's the breaks.

After Yeslick joins up and Eldoth whines at me, a guy named Rill comes up and asks me for 100 gold coins so he can bribe the captain of the guard in order to sneak his fellow slaves out of the mines before I murder them all with plug water. I acquiesce and emancipate his proclamation. He runs off to free his people, like a good little Moses.

I continue working my way through the mines, when I come upon a murder death kill room. There are corpses everywhere and the buzzing of flies echoes off the dark walls. An ogre mage appears and declares me a dead man.

I laugh, and Rasaad katana kills him.

Down, down, down.

We finally make it to the bottom of the mines, and a secret door reveals...BOSS FIGHT!

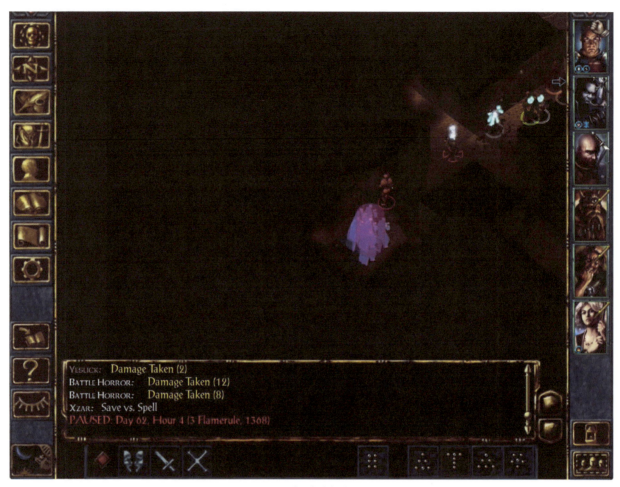

Funkadelic!

Evil baddy Davaeron appears and goes all pinky-purple with a Ghostbusters 2 slime wall protecting him while a bunch of guards and a few murder spells try to kill us. We fight them off and work away at Davaeron's funky fresh teleporting dance moves until he's all out of pink slime. After that, it just takes a few sword thwacks to take him down. We manage to kill him without anyone in our party dying, which is a good thing. I AM LEARNING.

He was a pain in the butt, though.

Anyway, I get a surprise cinematic telling me that I need to go to Baldur's Gate next.

Wait. What? You mean **the** Baldur's Gate? Really?

Finally. THE TITULAR CITY!

On my way out of the mines, I bump into Stephan, Davaeron's apprentice. I squeeze him for information by way of clicking various dialog options with impunity. He sings like an exposition canary, and I find out that the whole iron shortage was concocted by the Iron Throne in order to drive up demand so that they could then come in with their iron supplies and be the Big Dang Heroes and sell their stock at record profits. So basically, this game is the plot of Wall Street, but with swords. Neat, Bioware.

I let him live and catch an elevator back to the plug floor.

We pop the cork and flood the mine.

QUEST COMPLETE! And no sign of Imoen this time. Life is good.

Onward to Baldur's Gate!

We travel through the wilderness for ages until we get to a bridge leading to Baldur's Gate. We strut across it all heroically, but we're accosted by some guy named Scar who demands six gold pieces per party member for entry. He then insists that I investigate the suspicious death of someone named Mufasa. Or maybe it was some boring crap about a trading group short selling their assets and NO ONE CARES ABOUT THIS ECONOMIC NONSENSE. I tell the jerk what he wants to hear and he lets me in.

FINALLY!

Part Five
The Flaming Fists

We finally enter the city of Baldur's Gate. The fog of war is literally everywhere. I don't know where anything is, and I can't even see very far in front of my face. Has no one heard of a visitor's center in this place? A tourist map would go a long way.

I consult my journal, which is predictably useless, as usual. The main quest notes just basically say to GO TO BALDUR'S GATE AND DO A THING, so I guess that optional side quest from Scar is optionally mandatory, because I don't know what the hell else to do in this giant city. My journal entry for his quest tells me to go to the southwest corner of the city and investigate the Seven Suns, which totally sounds like a Heaven's Gate style cult. I guess I need to get there before they drink their cyanide Kool-Aid and go up to the alien mothership or whatever. Rasaad will probably love these people.

We take five steps, and Dorn pipes up about some other city called Lusker or something, and tells me how it's totally just like Baldur's Gate and some other things about his vengeance quest I don't care about. I just nod until he stops talking.

We press on.

We make it to the docks, and some creepy guy named Kesheel comes up to me out of nowhere, talking about how strolling along the docks is good for thinking. He then tells me what I think is supposed to be a joke about poop decks or something, and goes away.

Oh...kay...

A block later, another guy comes up to me, uninvited. This one is called Kerrachus, and he warns me about the dangers of slippery cobblestones and goes away. Good to know, dude.

We finally make it to the southwest corner of the city as instructed, and I still have no idea where to go, because the inky blackness of the accursed fog of war permeates my very soul. I wander all over the place for about half an hour, then finally find the Seven Suns building about 10 meters from where I first entered the stupid area.

Sigh.

We go inside. A merchant comes up to me and tells me the place has been overrun by shape-shifters because I guess whoever wrote this piece of garbage story was really into David Icke at the time. He has no other useful info, so we go upstairs.

There are several more merchants here, who all look and talk exactly the same, and say the exact same damn things whenever I talk to any of them. Maybe Icke has been right all along. I decide to keep my eye out for trans-dimensional reptilian alien overlords. Because you never know.

There's nothing upstairs, so I start pixel hunting until I find a door I missed back on the first floor. Except that it's actually more like stairs, which lead us down into the basement.

We are immediately attacked by something called a Doppelganger. We kill it and talk to some guy named Asshole, who turns out to be the leader of the Seven Suns and is being held captive by the shape-shifting goons.

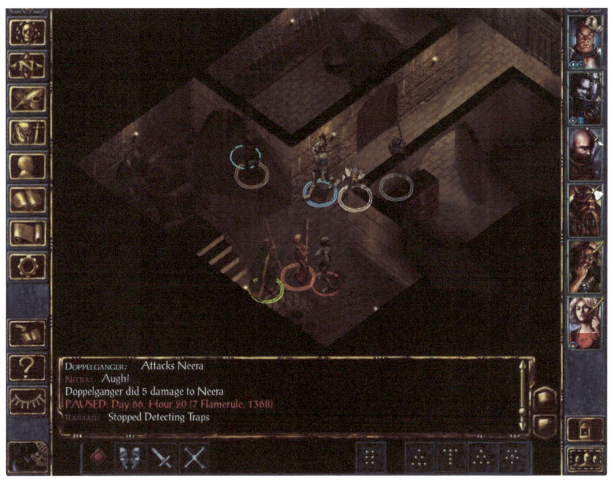

Icke was right!

Oops. Sorry. His name is actually Jhasso, but either moniker fits. He accuses us of being in league with the devil and talks about his noggin.

We assure him that we're quite nice people, actually, and tell him that Scar sent us for help with getting Simba to Pride Rock before the hyenas eat Nala and what does any of it matter, anyway? He just goes on about how the shape-shifters took over his business and drove profits into the ground. It's just more boring economic nonsense and I don't care anymore.

I end the conversation, and Jhasso runs off upstairs, emboldened by the one Doppelganger my weakling mage was able to kill by whacking it on the head twice with his walking stick, and vows to reclaim his business. What an Jhasshole.

We go back to the first floor, where the fat Santa-looking merchants from earlier suddenly all start attacking me, because they're actually Doppelgangers who apparently didn't at all care that the guy they've been holding prisoner in the basement for the past several months just ran past them on a holy quest to balance his checkbook or whatever. I kill them all.

We go upstairs and murder the merchant bastards up there, too. Because screw them.

We leave the building, and a guard walks up to tell me that I need to go see Scar over at the Flaming Fist headquarters building. Wherever the heck that is.

We go back to the bridge, but Scar isn't there. We then spend the next hour aimlessly wandering around the eleventy-hundred screens that make up the urban sprawl of this accursed city, only to finally find the damn Flaming Fist HQ was ALL THE WAY BACK IN THE SOUTHWEST CORNER WHERE I ALREADY WAS.

Sigh.

It starts raining. Dorn gets struck by lightning. No, really. He just shrugs it off and we push on. Badass.

We find Scar, and tell him that Timon and Pumbaa were really shape-shifters or whatever, and he pays us for our time before offering us another quest I don't give a crap about.

I decide to just wander around the city until we trigger the next story event.

We eventually stumble into the giant Iron Throne castle I didn't notice earlier, and some guy named Triadore comes running up to me, babbling about how he has no time to chit-chat, just before he starts chit-chatting with me. He tells me that there's madness here that he cannot stand any longer. FINALLY! Someone in this game I can agree with. I tell him to calm down, then he yells at me some more and leaves.

We wander deeper into the castle. A guard stops me and looks ready for a fight. I slip him 200 gold pieces, and he looks the other way. We head upstairs.

An archer named Dra'tan approaches me because you can't throw a rock in a fantasy world without hitting someone with ridiculous apostrophes in his name, and he asks me where I'm going. I tell him that we're on our way to the fifth floor to deliver a message to someone I don't know, which is risky because I've never been here before and I have no idea if there even is a fifth floor, but screw it. I live on the edge.

He buys my story, then warns me about more shape-shifters. Yay.

On the next floor, another guard accosts me. I bribe this one too, since I guess there's no such thing as an honest cop anymore, and we continue making our way upstairs.

We meet a bartender, who asks me if I want a drink. I tell him no, so he tries to murder me. Seems fair.

I murder him right back. And his little friends, too.

However, I start to get the nagging feeling that I shouldn't have done that, so I cast a magical fluxus capacitorus spell and reverse time with the Load Game button. We try again.

I ignore the bartender this time and go up to a little dude named Destus Gurn. Oh, boy. HE'S AN ACCOUNTANT. He throws a wall of text at me about trade negotiations and blah blah blah. I pick a random dialog option, and he tells me I can go upstairs.

Before I leave, I notice that there are a bunch of bookshelves here. I remember that jerk back in Candlekeep saying that I needed to bring him a book titled I don't know what, so I have Xzar steal every tome from this library. The right one is bound to be in there, somewhere.

We head upstairs, and some guy who sounds like Foghorn Leghorn tells me to fear his wrath, for it is great indeed, I do declare. I try to tell him that I'm someone else, but he sees through my clever little ruse and attacks. His friends rush to his aid.

Neera tries to put them to sleep, but fails. Xzar tries to horrify them, but isn't scary at all today. Things go badly.

I reload.

The fight is intense, but we eventually win. I lose my mages and the monk with the Kung Fu grip, but I'll resurrect them at a temple soon enough. No big deal. Meanwhile, one of the Iron Throne leaders tells me that the REAL bad guys are back in Candlekeep. Who could have foreseen this?!

I let him live and find a bunch more books in a cabinet. I steal them before I leave.

We walk outside, and a city guard tells me that Scar wants to see me again, but I've no time for Needy Nellies. Instead, I head to the nearest temple and resurrect my slightly-less-useless-than-they-were-before companions, and we ready ourselves for battle.

TO CANDLEKEEP!

We arrive and saunter confidently up to the jerk who wouldn't let us in earlier. However, despite carrying AN ENTIRE LIBRARY'S WORTH OF BOOKS with me, I apparently DON'T HAVE THE RIGHT ONE, so I still can't go in.

FINE. I guess talking to Scar again was important, after all. I hope so, anyway. Because if he doesn't have whatever this magical mystery book is, I'm screwed. I don't know where to find it, or even have any idea what it's called.

Back to Baldur's Gate!

We fast travel back to the Flaming Fist headquarters, murdering anyone and anything foolish enough to waylay us along the way. My party starts griping at me about needing rest, but screw them. Ain't nobody got time for that. They can sleep the next time they die and I don't resurrect their sorry butts. That crap's getting expensive.

I talk to Scar, who refuses to help me because I haven't bothered investigating whatever other crap he wanted me to look into that I assumed was optional, but I guess isn't. I poke around the Flaming Fist HQ for a while, hoping to find the secret book of wonders hiding somewhere, but come up empty. We're on our way out when Scar approaches us again.

He tells me not to bother with that other thing that was super important five seconds ago, and tells me that Duke Ellington wants to see me about the Iron Throne. We go meet him.

The Duke of Earl then asks me to investigate the Iron Throne that I've already investigated, then commands me to report back to him with the findings I've already found. He offers to pay me 2,000 gold pieces for my trouble, then ends the conversation.

I start it back up again and tell him that I've already done all that shit and to show me the money. He tells me I need to go back to Candlekeep, which I already know, but then he GIVES ME THE BOOK OF SECRETS! This little bastard was just sitting on it the whole time. Jerk.

I get a quick little cinematic with a picture of a book titled Baldur's Gate while I'm in a city named Baldur's Gate and playing a game called Baldur's Gate. OMG, SO META!

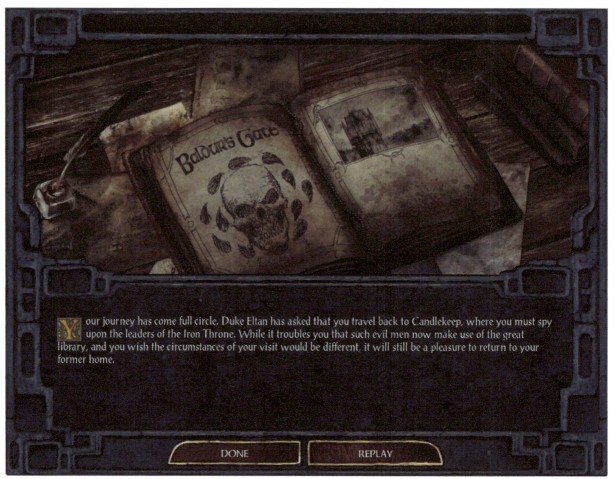

It's a game within a game within a game...

After the little scene, the game dumps me back outside Candlekeep, where I drop all of the useless books I've been lugging around for absolutely no reason, and I free up a ton of inventory pockets in my pants. I walk up to the fathead at the gate.

"Oy! Fathead! I've got yer book, ya miserable old bastard."

He lets me in.

We make our way to the central Keep and start climbing the stairs. Every now and then, we're stopped by some old friend or another who I don't even know, but who tells me what a great boy I was growing up, and how everyone loves me but screw you if you come back home without a book we want, you wretched little orphan. Whatever. We keep climbing.

Eventually, we find the Big Bad Guy named Realtor or something. Probably goes back to the whole economics plot of the game, maybe something to do with a property scheme. Forget it, Jake. This is Baldurtown.

Anyway, he mocks us, so we murder him. And a bunch of his friends. WE HAVE SAVED THE DAY!

For our efforts, we're thrown in jail. Because of course we are.

We're just chilling in our spacious cell when some guy in a red robe swings by and totally doesn't believe that we're bad guys because he remembers me from when I was a little tyke and used to pee in the town fountain or something. I don't care. He teleports us away to the secret catacombs beneath the Keep, and we make our escape.

We're attacked by a woman named Phlydia, who thinks we stole her book. We probably did, though. I've lost track of all the crap I've nicked since this whole mess started, so we kill her and move on. She was a Doppelganger anyway, so who really cares?

The catacombs go on for days and are trapped to all hell and back. We "explore" the entirety of the labyrinthine nightmare, only to find that the exit was pretty much right next to the entrance.

Sigh.

We leave. Or, at least, I thought we were leaving. Apparently, there are multiple levels to these catacombs. OH, JOY.

I kill a few guys, slap around a bunch of skeletons, then quicksave and rest. I'm greeted with a dream sequence that usually signifies the end of a chapter. THANK GOD.

I wake everyone up, and we move on. We run into a guy named Elminster, who's dressed like Rincewind from Discworld. I accuse him of being a Doppelganger, but he says, "Nuh-uh! Am not!" so I'm like, "Oh, okey dokey, then. I believe you!"

I tell him that I'll follow him out of the catacombs, and he leads us onward. We start walking past some monsters, but Elminster Rincewind doesn't seem at all concerned. I start to wonder about his lackadaisical attitude toward our imminent peril, when suddenly...yeah, he's totally a Doppelganger. And so are his friends.

FIGHT!

Xzar and Neera put most of the little buggers to sleep, but Elminster is apparently a Greater Doppelganger, which I guess means he's immune to nappy time or something. We punch him to death and leave.

We emerge into a cave system that's above the catacombs, but below the Keep. Which makes total sense in this place of insanity.

We then run into a guy named Prat, who turns out to be a total badass, despite his stupid name. He kills us all. Repeatedly. I try sending my entire party after him as a distraction, hoping to run away to the exit while they all die in agony for the greater good, but the caves are filled with all sorts of nasty monsters that chop, slice, bite, and/or explode my insides before I can get very far.

This is going to require some effort.

And we were so close!

Part Six
I'm Finally Finished

I managed to cast Horror on some of Prat the prat's friends, and we killed him a lot. Once he was dead, we ran away while his horrified buddies were busy pooping in their loincloths.

Then, we ran into basilisks and were turned to stone. And we died. A lot. Like, seriously. A lot.

I search through all my spells, and I don't have any anti-petrification anything, not that it matters because petrification is apparently instadeath. Which is really annoying when I get hit and immediately die, then have to sit and wait for the stupid dead hand animation to play over and over and over again.

We go back up to where Prat was, and start picking off his friends one by one, who are now scattered all around the caves. We murder some spiders while we're hunting them down, but none of them - even the mages - have a protection from petrification spell, which I learned is a thing that exists because I CONSULTED THE MANUAL. Again.

So I go back and try to fight the basilisks some. I manage to make it through once, but my entire party gets turned to stone and is dead to me, which I figure might make the endgame a little too difficult.

I reload and try again. And again. I manage to kill the little bastards, but Neera dies. She's finally a decent mage at this point, and I hate to lose her. So I reload and try again. And again. And again.

I could really us the Sword of Gryffindor right about now.

I'm about to give up, when I go digging through my characters' inventories, looking for anything that might help me. I find a quiet spot in the caves, load the mages up with Identify spells and rest a bunch of times, because spiders keep waking us up. Eventually, they sleep long enough to learn the spells by whatever magical, scroll-under-the-pillow brain osmosis they're using, and I make them start identifying every unknown thing we own.

Which is a lot of stuff, because we haven't had a chance to find a good resting spot since we stormed the Candlekeep Keep. I find some scrolls in Yeslick's pockets and Xzar identifies them. Turns out, the little bastard was sitting on a Protection From Petrification scroll all this time.

Of course, no one in my party can actually learn the spell for some unknown reason handed down by the freaking AD&D Lawgivers, but whatever. I cast it on myself and charge the basilisks alone.

They try their best to turn me to stone, but since I'm immune to that trickery, they've lost their nuclear option. I wail on them with my +1 Long Sword until they're basilisk pudding. I call out to the useless fatheads to come join me, now that the danger is over.

They come running. We continue onward, toward where I hope the exit is.

We run into a guy named Diarmid, who thinks I'm Prat because I guess evil henchmen lackeys don't get invited to company picnics, so they've never met each other in person. He tells me that we must not keep whatever the hell The Sarevok is waiting, and laughs about how we got that poor guy Jeet locked up. (That's me, by the way. Just in case you're a little slow on the uptake.)

He thinks everything went as planned, so I tip my hat and tell him good day, then get ready to stab him in his miserable back the second he lets us walk past him. Yeah, it's like that, dude. You lock me up in jail, you get prison rules. Deal with it.

Except I never get the chance, because the little weasel hightails it out of there like his hair's on fire.

We exit the caves, and I get a new little cutscene that tells me I have to go back to Baldur's Gate again, because what would an adventure be without the indescribable joy of incessant backtracking. I have to hunt down whoever this Sarevok person is.

Fine. Let's do this. To Baldur's Gate! AGAIN!

But first, I decide to get some rest before we try to fast travel and end up being waylaid by +10 Ogres Of Malfeasance or something. We light up a campfire, bust out the marshmallows and tell ghost stories until we drift off to dreamland.

That's when a giant, skull-faced baboon with horns shows up. It's another one of these damn dream visions I keep getting that mostly consist of pretty bad narration and a wall of text. Apparently, the blood of someone called Bhaal runs through my veins and has something to do with my origins that I was either never told about, or wasn't paying any attention when I was. It could go either way, really.

Anyway, evil baboon dude is Sarevok, I guess. And I need to go kill him. FOR REASONS.

onight, you sleep hunted by all and wake in a dream hunted by one.

Tonight you are the monster everyone claims you are: the kobold scorned like a rodent, the ogre that children fear comes in the night. The mobs and their torches now come for you, counting you among the creatures you once did hunt. Or so someone would have you believe.

Once again you hear the voice, a voice that now makes no secret of its origins. It speaks of destiny and nature, and of evils bred in the bone. It says you will never be free of the mob, that they will hunt you for what you are. Murder and death run through your heart, and accepting that will supposedly give you power. The essence of Bhaal within you cannot be ignored.

| REPLAY | DONE |

Behold! The muppet baboon...OF DOOM!

Awakened from our momentary slumber, we find ourselves getting griped at by a guard for sleeping out in the open. He tells me to go to the Inn if I need to sleep and not, you know, back to the prison cell where I'm supposed to be right now since everyone thinks I've gone on a murder rampage across the Sword Coast. But hey, whatever. This guard's cool. He's not going to bust us.

We try to go to the Inn and crash for the night, but we're outside of the town walls and that jerk at the gate won't let me in again unless I bring him another stupid book.

FINE. Screw you guys, we're leaving. We'll just sleep whenever we get to Baldur's Gate, and my companions can crywhine about being tired all they want because I just don't give a damn anymore. We'll find an Inn when we get there, then go to sleep and wake up the next morning, ready to complete the final and epic chapter in my battle against whatever the hell has been going on all this time.

ONWARD!

We get a good night's rest in the most expensive suite at the Blade and Stars because why the hell not, we've earned it. I check my journal, which tells me to GO BACK TO BALDUR'S GATE AND DO ANOTHER THING that I don't know what it is, so I guess that means it's time for more directionless wandering. VERY HOORAY.

I mosey about the city for a while, just walking around and enjoying the sites like some kind of tourist because I don't really know what the hell else to do. We're busy movin' on up to the East Side and looking for a deluxe apartment in the sky high, high when a guy named Marek comes up and harshes our mellow.

"Could we have a moment of your time?" he asks. Uh oh. The royal We. No good can ever come of it.

I ask him what he wants. He tells me that he and his companion, a presumably invisible dude I can't see named Lothander, work for the Iron Throne, and they would very much like it if I would stop murdering all their friends, please and thank you.

I tell him to get stuffed and get ready for a fight that never happens because they just disappear. Weird place, this city.

We walk a little farther, then some lunatic yells, "I SURV THA FLAMIN' FIST" in what I can only assume is the equivalent of whatever a Texas accent is in the Forgotten Realms universe. He calls me a murderer since the whole world is against me now I guess, because I'm the hero Baldur's Gate deserves, but not the one it needs. I murder him in the face.

My reputation goes down, but what do I care? Everyone who's never even heard of me has turned against us, so I don't really give a damn what they think.

We press on.

I run into a guy name Delthyr, who tells me he represents "those who harp". I have no idea what that means, but I'm assuming he's talking about those women who play unobtrusive music in the corners of fancy wedding receptions. Or maybe he's talking about people who drone on and on about the same thing, day after day, month after month until you finally just want to tell Gary that no, your stupid fascination with that television show you love is of no interest to me or anyone else and I swear to god, if you make that joke with the coffee pot one more time, I'm going to cut you and leave your body out by the dumpster for the dogs to choke on, you miserable, brown-nosing loser.

Wait. Sorry. I kind of blacked out for a second there. Anyway, Delthyr here represents those who harp, whatever that means and I don't care. He tells me that Scar was assassinated, and Duke Ferdinand has come down with a mysterious illness and is probably about to die. He also says I've been accused of murder like I didn't already know, and that Sarevok is the new Iron Throne president. Oh, and the Flaming Fist has a warrant out for my arrest, which explains all the fisters I've been murdering in the streets.

Delthyr walks away, then another exposition bot named Tamoko comes up and tells me that the healer curing Duke Wellington isn't a healer at all. MOAR PLOT TWIST!

Ah, screw all of this. I'm tired and just want it to end. All of it. We decide to storm the Flaming Fist Castle and damn the torpedoes. If we're going out, we're going in a blaze of flaming, fisting glory.

CHARGE!

I'm in the middle of storming the castle and murdering fisters when Tamoko pops up out of freaking nowhere and demands that I not kill Sarevok. She says she wants to help him live his life as a man, not as the god he thinks he can be. I suspect this will lead to the Good Bioware Ending, so yeah. That's not going to happen. I tell her to piss off, and I return to swinging my big ass sword at the bad guy in front of me.

We make our way into the castle and are immediately attacked by all the everyone. It's a tough battle, but we manage to murder them all, then head upstairs to finish the job.

Clark Kent is waiting for us. He's a former fister who remembers me from when I helped Scar all those many, like, few hours ago. But he's had enough of the new leadership and wants out. He warns me that the healer in the next room isn't a healer at all, which I already knew, then runs off to a phone booth somewhere. Or possibly Kansas.

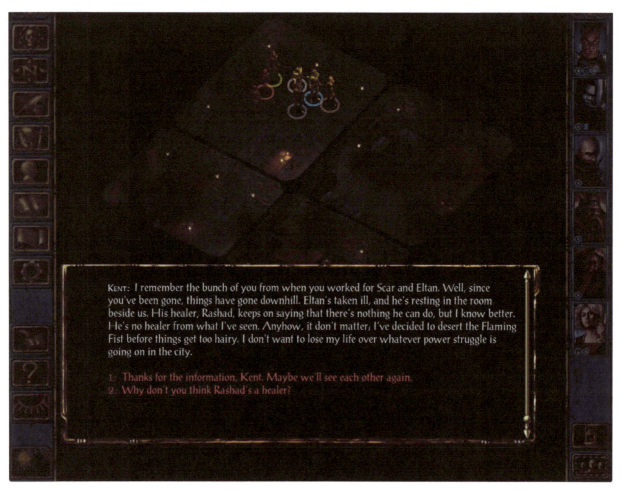

KENT: I remember the bunch of you from when you worked for Scar and Eltan. Well, since you've been gone, things have gone downhill. Eltan's taken ill, and he's resting in the room beside us. His healer, Rashad, keeps on saying that there's nothing he can do, but I know better. He's no healer from what I've seen. Anyhow, it don't matter; I've decided to desert the Flaming Fist before things get too hairy. I don't want to lose my life over whatever power struggle is going on in the city.

1: Thanks for the information, Kent. Maybe we'll see each other again.
2: Why don't you think Rashad's a healer?

The Forgotten Realms: Smallville Edition

We walk in and surprise Rashad by stabbing at him with pointy things until he dies. Before he shuffles off this mortal coil, he reveals himself to be a Greater Doppelganger, shocking no one.

After we're done murdering Rashad, we wake up The Duke and tell him hush now, baby. Everything's going to be alright. Daddy's here. He looks at us like we're crazy, but then just goes with it and asks me to carry him to the Harbor Master's building, wherever that is. He coughs a bunch, then tells me that I need to find Slyth and the Family Stone, and someone named Krystin before Sarevok turns everything to crap.

I stuff him into one of my inventory pockets, and we make haste to the Harbor Master's building, which I'm guessing is somewhere by the harbor.

QUICKLY! TO THE DOCKS!

But first, we stop off at a nearby Inn to try and get some rest because it's a pain in the ass that this whole endgame takes place inside the city, where the damn guards won't let you sleep outside. However, when I go into the Inn, the innkeeper turns me away because he's freaking Yoda or something and senses evil in me, which he'll have none of in his fine establishment, thankyouverymuch.

Fine. Whatever, dude. We're outta here. We didn't want to stay in your stupid hotel anyway. Jerk.

We fast travel out of the city, sleep in the woods, then head back to the docks. The second we step foot into the area, some dude named Kolvar runs up to tell me that The Black Network sends its regards, whoever the hell they are. He then tells me everything I already know about the Iron Throne and Sarevok and the little dying Duke I have in my pocket. I guess he was the backup exposition guy, just in case I went to the docks before I went to the Flaming Fist.

He wanders off, then we make our way to the Harbor Master's building. Of course, everyone is bitching at me about being tired again, because it apparently takes EIGHT FREAKING HOURS to travel outside the city walls and back in again, so everyone is already sleepy after we just sneaked outside to sleep. Whatever. I gotta do something about this Duke in my pocket. He's creating an unsightly bulge.

I whip him out and give him to the Harbor Master, who scurries off into the darkness. I guess that wraps that up, then. Nothing left to do now but storm the Iron Throne and murder the crap out of Sarevok.

TO BATTLE!

Or, more accurately, TO WALKING! And being talked to by a whole bunch of rats fleeing a sinking ship. Apparently, the other members of the Iron Throne have had enough of whatever it is Sarevok has been doing, and they're all shipping out on the next boat to anywhere but here. Can't say as I blame them, either. I'm about to paint the walls with some blood up in here.

We make our way to the fifth floor, where some woman named Cythandria starts shouting at me about how she's Sarevok's lover and that I'm gonna be real sorry and so on. She also says I share some sort of "true" heritage with Sarevok, because it wouldn't be a hero myth without a MYSTERIOUS ORIGIN, so I'm probably Voldemort's final horcrux. I'm fine with that.

She puts up her dukes. Let's do this.

I rush her, but she has two giant friends appear out of nowhere. We make a break for the stairs, and head down to the bar where we pick off Ughh and the other Ughh without Cythandira's magic getting in the way. Once they're dead, we head back up for the witch or concubine, or whatever the hell she is.

We beat the crap out of each other for a while, before she eventually cries uncle and begs me not to kill her. She tells me that Sarevok is hiding out in the Undercellar, which I can get to through the sewers. Because of course, we have to go to the sewers. What kind of roleplaying game would be complete without a trek through some dumb sewers?

I let her live, though. Because I'm a gentleman.

We leave the Iron Throne castle and hop down the nearest sewer grate. It's time to end this.

Healing spells cast on rest until fully healed.
Quick Save successful.
Jeet: It shall be as you wish.
The journey took 4 hours.
Jeet: I shall attend to it in a trice.

Sewers. Why did there have to be sewers?

We roam around the sewers for hours, killing gelatinous bits of goo called Mustard Jelly or something, talk to a few rats that go squeak, get prophesied on by the Sewer King, and murder the entire Ratchild kobold gang. Eventually, we meander down yet another identical tunnel and emerge in some kind of brothel. In the sewers. Sounds hygienic.

Slyth and Krystin are here, and I kill them for having stupid names. After they're dead, I search their corpses. Slyth was carrying an invitation to the Ducal Palace, so I guess that's where we're headed next.

I find an exit from the brothel, but we're stopped by a guard who demands 10 gold pieces from each of us before he'll allow us to enter the place we're already in. We pay him just to avoid any unpleasantness, then promptly leave.

We pop up inside an Inn where the owners don't think I'm an evil bastard, so I rent a room and let everyone get some rest so they'll stop bitching at me about being exhausted. We awake refreshed and ready for more murder.

Next stop, the palace!

We make our way to the palace, but keep running into Flaming Fist zealots along the way, which sucks because I can't kill any more of them, or else most of my goody-two-shoes companions will leave me because they don't want to work for a murderer. Well, a mass murderer, anyway. Semantics.

I just keep quick saving, reloading, and doing my best to avoid confrontation as we make our way to the palace.

Finally, we approach the palace gates and are met by a guy named Bill, who asks to see our invitations. I show him the pages we ripped off the cold, dead body of Slyth. He doesn't seem to mind the blood stains, and lets us in.

Once inside, another Flaming Fist yahoo yells his stupid Texan battlecry and demands to see our invitations again. We give them to him, and he leaves us alone. Lot of security in this place.

When we walk into the main room, some mucky muck named Lila Jannath starts speaking. And I mean, with actual speech. There's so little in the way of voice work in this game, I can only assume this means shit's about to get real.

I get ready to kill. But first, I have to sit through a lot of bickering nobles, before Sarevok finally chimes in. He blames all the world's problems on everyone but himself, then moves to America and the Tea Party elects him President. Or they probably would, if I didn't stop him right here and now. For freedom.

But first, I have to deal with all the people who just turned into Greater Doppelgangers. And by deal with, I mean murder with extreme prejudice. I'm in the middle of disemboweling one of them when Sarevok pauses the action to call me an assassin, then instructs all of the people who are already trying to kill me to, I dunno, kill me harder or something, I guess.

I eventually finish off the last one, then some guy named Belt thanks me for saving his life and he is eternally grateful and whatnot. This pisses Sarevok off something fierce, and he comes at me with his spiky horn helmet.

Bring it on.

He farts all over the damn room and nearly kills us with his gas cloud. And here I was thinking I was about to have an epic confrontation with the Dark Lord. Instead, I get freaking Pig Pen from the Peanuts gang. Fine. Whatever.

We wail on each other and I gag on his stink cannon for a while, until he eventually chickens out and runs away. Belt comes up to me and tells me that the only way to end this is to end this, so I give him a gold star for obviousness, and he teleports us to the Thieves' Guild.

The thieves tell us that Sarevok came storming through only moments ago, and tore off down the stairs. We take off after him.

Descending into the basement, I come across an injured little…thing called Voleta Stiletto. She or he, or whatever it is tells me that Sarevok has gone into a mother humping maze, which just freaking figures. It's not enough that I've thought this game was over three different times already, but now there's a damn maze to contend with.

WHAT NEXT IN THE PARADE OF CONSTANT AGGRAVATION?!

Fine, then. I guess we'll be maze runners.

Sigh.

I cast the bones and summon the ancient oracle of Googleardium Leviosa to guide me through the maze. (In the common tongue, that means I looked up a map on the internet because screw you; I don't do video game mazes.)

We make our way to the exit, killing various beasties and setting off a bunch of traps on the way that Imoen wouldn't have bothered to notice had she been here anyway, so I don't feel the least bit bad about leaving her wherever the hell I left her. I hope she died screaming.

Lying near death at the exit is a guy named Winski Perorate, who was apparently Sarevok's mentor or something. He tells me that we are of the same blood and a whole bunch of other stuff I'm too worn out from trudging through this maze to bother reading, so I click out of the conversation and leave him to rot.

We exit the maze into a cave of some sort, or possibly an underground graveyard. I have no idea where I am anymore. We plod along for a brief walk before we're set upon by other Iron Throne board members who are pissed about their stock options or something. I explain to them that I'm trying to take Sarevok down, but they don't give a crap and just start slinging spells at me.

We get our butts kicked a few times, but Yeslick eventually manages to silence their mages before one of them can launch what I can only describe as a thermonuclear magic death missile, and they go down pretty easily after that.

We loot their corpses and push on. The Tomako girl from earlier appears out of nowhere again, and she still doesn't want us to kill Saverok. We tell her that we still do want to kill Sarevok. She tells us that now she wants to kill me, so I kill her and move on with my life.

We stand ready at the doors of some dark temple.

LET THIS BE OUR FINAL BATTLEFIELD!

We throw open the doors and rush inside, where every bad guy starts casting protection spells. That can't be good.

Within seconds, the spells start flying. Sarevok shouts at me, and a couple of his allies materialize in Ghostbusters slime and start flinging death balls at me. My mages fling death balls right back at them.

Sarevok uses his ungodly fart power, and we're caught in the cloud. We retreat, killing one of his allies along the way. Probably confused because someone forgot to program an AI subroutine to counteract my strategy of Not Knowing What The Hell I'm Doing, Sarevok's other allies don't bother with me after that. Instead, Sarevok himself sprints over to me and starts bashing my head with his sword.

I bash him right back, while Xzar and Neera throw magic missiles at his face. Rasaad is five-point-palm exploding his heart all over the place, while Yeslick is shouting something in dwarfish and Dorn is…doing whatever it is Dorn does. This goes on for a few minutes, with a few healing spells tossed for good measure, when suddenly…SAREVOK IS DEFEATED. The game is won!

It is over. I'm finally Finished.

I can hold my head up high, now that I've finally completed this game after 16 years of not giving a crap about it. I still don't quite understand what all the fuss is about, though. It's not a bad game, but it's certainly not a great one, either.

For now, I will say that I eventually ended up having a lot more fun with Baldur's Gate than I ever thought I would going in. Sure, it took me over half the game to get there, but once I did, I enjoyed playing it more often than I didn't. Except for the sewers and the mazes and all the stupid bits, of course.

The game created a final save file for me when I killed the Big Bad, which I eventually imported into Baldur's Gate 2 to start this whole crazy trip all over again. But more on that in the next Interlude.

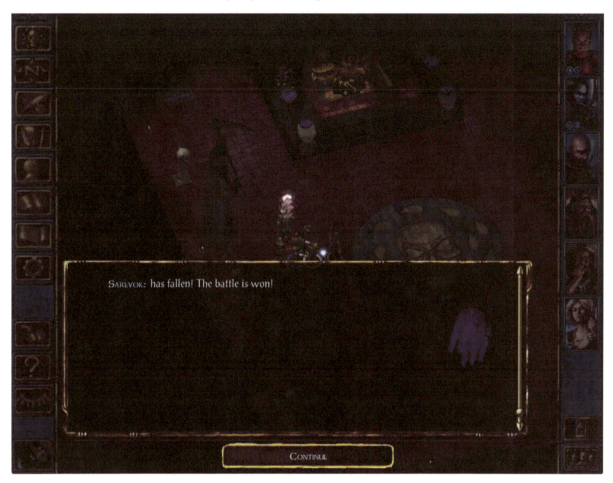

It is done.

Chapter Four

Enter middle school in the '80s, otherwise known as Lord of the Flies with Izods and Swatch watches. Sixth grade was a pretty terrible year for me, which is saying something considering most of middle school was a never-ending parade of unrelenting sorrow, but I made some new and lasting friends who were on the nerdier side of the social spectrum, and that was fine by me. One friend in particular - his name was Mark - even had a laptop. A LAPTOP!

In truth, it was more of a "portable computer" in the same sense that almost anything is portable as long as you can put wheels on it and have a vehicle powerful enough to pull it a few feet. It was a monster of a thing, really. The screen was some sort of Neolithic LCD affair, all monochromatic and impossibly slow. I'm not sure if it technically even had a refresh rate, but if it did, it was less interested in Hertz as a frequency and more in Hertz as the rental car company. But only very slow and unreliable rental cars. It was the broken down Pinto of monitors.

Anyway, we were playing around with it one day when he showed me the most amazing thing my young eyes had ever seen. He pulled the phone cord out of his football phone (whimsically shaped phones were an '80s thing best not reflected too deeply upon today) and plugged it into the computer. WHAT SORCERY WAS THIS?!

He pushed a few buttons, and a minute later the machine began to emit these strange mating calls of antediluvian god-beasts, until they were eventually silenced and replaced by words on the screen...

Welcome To CrazyBBS!

I was enthralled.

It was an electronic Bulletin Board System, and my first exposure to a brave new world that would eventually become the internet, right there on that tiny, terrible little screen. He showed me message boards and ASCII games called Doors, file shares, and messaging. It was amazing, and I was amazed by it.

Then, he pushed a button to page someone called a sysop (pronounced sis-op, and I'll hear no more on the subject from you sci-sop buffoons, *thankyouverymuch*). A moment or two later, the screen wiped (ok, that took more than a few moments, since the magical little gnome inside the wonder box had to erase and redraw the screen with his tiny little gnome hands), and someone named Pebbles started to chat with us.

She was a girl.

A girl our age.

As soon as we were done chatting with her, Mark unplugged the phone line from the computer and back into his football phone. Then, I immediately called my Mom to ask if I could spend the night. And the rest is history.

(*Sidenote*: I don't actually believe he had a football phone, now that I'm thinking about it. But I had one shaped like a frog, so it'll do for the sake of Painting A Mind Picture For You. So shut up.)

I became obsessed with BBSs after that. I begged and pleaded with my parents to buy me a modem, which eventually paid off when my birthday came around. That January, I made a wish, blew out some candles, and unwrapped the most beautiful package I had ever held.

Three hundred bauds of pure telecommunicative bliss.

Of course, in these modern times of broadband and cell phone data plans, 300 baud seems quaint. And maybe it was, but I didn't care. Sure, it was slower than delivering data packets by way of hopping on a Big Wheel and 360-spinning your way down the street to your friend's house, but it was magical. For the first time, I didn't have to be a scrawny little nerdboy. I could be whoever I wanted, and as long as I could type convincingly, people would never even know that I was a little five pound nothing of a child.

So I learned to type. Fast. Very fast. But I developed my own system, which would later come to haunt me in typing classes when I would get into heated arguments with the teachers regarding their inefficient and ridiculous keyboarding rules taught unchanged from 1943. But they would eventually shut up and go away once I'd demonstrated how much better my method was by way of typing a whole lot faster than they could, and I'd be left alone for the rest of the semester. Which was nice.

So anyway, I learned to type fast. And smart. (At least for a dumb kid.) I developed a better vocabulary and learned the rules of grammar, not to get good grades on some pointless test in school, but so that I could pass for Not A Stupid Kid on BBSs. And it worked.

I desperately wanted to run my own BBS, but my Franklin didn't have a hard drive and I didn't have a dedicated phone line. I shared a line with my sister which was originally a pretty sweet deal for her since I didn't have many friends who would ever call me, so it was basically *her* phone line for years…until I got the modem.

After that, I was always on it, which infuriated her. Of course, it was pretty easy to get me off of the line by simply picking up the phone because it would disconnect me immediately, but those were the risks you took back in the day.

None of that stopped me from listing my number on local BBSs as my own BBS even though I didn't even have any software to run it. Instead, what I would do was wait for the phone to ring, then pick it up and see if it the squealing was coming from a teenage girl or another computer, and type the command for my machine to answer the call if it was for me. (The teenage girls were never for me.)

Since I was only running a basic terminal, I would then try my best to recreate the BBS experience by way of typing really fast and faking it. And I didn't even have to type all the fast really, because we're talking 300 baud here. Most people today can type faster than it could transmit characters, so I was actually fairly convincing. Right up until people realized I had no message boards or files sections or doors or anything at all that a standard BBS had to offer. I only had chat, which is why I would quickly recreate the "Sysop has broken into chat" dialog as soon as I was done "drawing" the welcome screen.

People caught on pretty fast.

Those were happy times for me. I made some great online friends, met interesting people, and made a lot of useful connections over the years that I would later learn is called "networking" and is something that responsible grown-ups supposedly do. But all I knew then was that I was talking to people who took me seriously, and I loved it.

Bulletin boards would stay with me through the rest of the '80s and well into the '90s, until the dot com boomed and the internet became a viable thing. So don't worry, they're hardly making their last appearance in this book. This is just how I dipped my first toe into the turbulent waters of online living. Of course, I eventually had to say goodbye to my 300 baud modem and get with the times.

Which led me to getting my first IBM-compatible PC: an 8088 with a 10-megabyte hard drive, an EGA monitor AND a Turbo Boost button. I was hot stuff.

But before that happened - between my glory days with the Apple][and my first PC - a little Japanese playing card company changed everything.

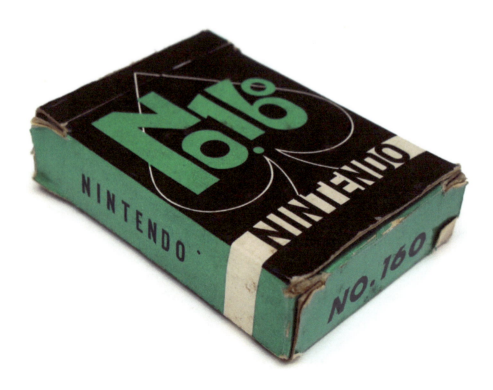

Chapter Five

I got my first Nintendo in either '85 or '86. I can't remember exactly which year, because you just don't pay close attention to time when you're a kid since you have so damn much of it. It's not until you get older and start noticing how much more sand is in the bottom of the hourglass than the top that you begin keeping track of all the individual grains. Or something like that, anyway.

I played with the NES off and on throughout my childhood, but I only have a couple of standout memories involving the console. The first one involves a guy named David, who was my best friend at the time and who now goes by Dave for some reason. And my own NES isn't even part of this story, since I didn't have one at the time.

I was hanging out over at his house one day when he showed me this cool new game he had called The Legend of Zelda. It was an amazing thing to behold, all golden and glistening in the moonlight. (Except the moonlight was just a normal incandescent light bulb illuminating an already lit bedroom in the middle of the afternoon in a suburban neighborhood, but just shut up and let me set the scene.)

Now, I'd been playing RPGs for a while at this point, but I'd never played anything like Zelda before. It was half Nintendo game, half RPG. Or maybe half Nintendo game, one-fourth RPG and one-fourth Adventure Game. It really doesn't matter because I've never been very good at fractions, but what it did was take a little bit of computer game magic and sprinkle it into a console game. THAT YOU COULD SAVE.

You see, up until Zelda, games reset every time you turned the console off. There was no such thing as Save Anywhere back in those days because it was all Save Nowhere until Zelda came along. It really was a revolutionary thing, to be able to save your progress in a console game. Before Zelda, the closest you could get was writing down an impossibly long "password" or "code" when you quit a game that you could then come back and put in the next time you wanted to play that would kinda/sorta pick up where you left off. But not really.

Zelda changed all that. You could save exactly where you were and what you were doing, along with your inventory and stats and all that good stuff. But there was also a problem with it, especially if you weren't familiar with the idea that you could actually save a console game. And *especially* especially if you were easily confused by the often questionable Japanese-English translations of early games.

Which is how it all went wrong...

So I was over at David - I mean Dave's - house, and he was showing me this really cool new game called Zelda. He took me through a bit of a dungeon and showed me how to fight Octoroks and plant bombs to blow up hidden passageways to secret rooms, and all sorts of fun stuff. Then, he quit his game, handed me the controller, and left the room.

And I was left sitting there, looking at the screen.

At the bottom, there was a little something that read ELIMINATION MODE. Now, what do you suppose that meant, exactly? Because to 10 or 11 year old me, that meant something amazing. Probably. I'm not sure I remember exactly what I thought it meant at the time, but from what I can recall, I believe it had something to do with me thinking that messing around with ELIMINATION MODE would let me increase Link's ability to ELIMINATE THINGS. I guess I thought it was a stat screen or something. Maybe I thought it was an arena mode where I could just go fight endless waves of monsters. Like I said, I don't remember exactly. I was a dumb kid who just pretended to be smart on what would eventually become the internet. Leave me alone.

Anyway, what ended up happening was that I selected ELIMINATION MODE and then used it on the Link character my friend had probably already spent hours upon hours playing, presumably to buff his stats or whatever the heck I was thinking it would do. But it didn't actually do anything like that. Nope, what ELIMINATION MODE actually did was DELETE THE SAVED GAME I DIDN'T EVEN KNOW EXISTED.

I guess Nintendo of America hadn't bothered to figure out what Delete meant yet, so they just ran the original Japanese through whatever the 1980s equivalent of Google Translate was (probably a guy named Steve down in Accounting or something), and just dumped the results out on the screen with nary a second thought.

This actually happened a lot, back in the olden times of yore. Some of the poor translation jobs have even been picked up by pop culture and are part of the non-gamer lexicon now. Things like, "Someone set us up the bomb" and "All your base are belong to us" are pretty much universally understood now, but they weren't then.

Just like ELIMINATION MODE wasn't. Which is how I ended up wiping my friend's saved game and then shutting off his NES in a panic when I realized what I'd done. I don't remember what happened after that, but I probably experienced a sudden drop in my desire to play video games and we went outside and rode our bikes or something. Like cave people.

The other main memory of the NES I have is buying games from Toys 'R Us. Back in the '80s, there was a giant wall dedicated to nothing but NES games at the biggest little toy store there was. But it didn't actually contain any games. What it had was a picture of the front and (if you were lucky) the back of the box, with a stack of little paper ticket things underneath. The idea was that you'd grab the ticket for whichever game you wanted, which you would then take to the nice teenager working behind the bulletproof pawn shop deathglass cage near the front of the store, who would then match your ticket with the proper game and sell it to you.

Also around this time, game shows for kids were beginning to get popular. Often, the grand prize on these shows would be a Toys 'R Us shopping spree, with the idea being that you would get five minutes to run all around the store, stuffing your cart with as many toys as you could before time ran out. And it was a sucker's game.

But I had a Plan. If I ever went on one of those game shows, my young prepubescent mind would conspire, I would know *exactly* what to do. I'd ignore all the stupid plastic toys and gewgaws that so entranced the insipid shoelickers of my peers, and go straight for the holy grail of the game aisle. And that's when I would bankrupt the store.

I reasoned that I could probably pull every ticket for every game off that wall in five minutes, with time to spare. Then, I'd be left with 50 copies of every NES game available, 49 of which I would sell at cut rates to friends and family out of the trunk of my dad's car. I would have every game I ever wanted **and** get rich while doing it. It was the perfect plan.

Of course, I never got a chance to test that theory, because I never made it on one of those shows. The closest I ever came to anything like that was being featured for all of five seconds on The New Mickey Mouse Club, where I barked like a dog for reasons unknown to me other than that some crew member shoved me in front of a camera and told me to when I was at Disney World one summer. And I never even saw it when it came on, nor have I ever seen it to this day.

But that didn't mean kids at school wouldn't see it, though. Because they did.

Did I mention how much I hated middle school?

Because I hated it a lot.

Chapter Six

Everything has been leading up to this. Seriously, the previous five chapters were just setting the stage for The Big Picture. Or at least that's what I'm telling myself. I just had to introduce the various highways and byways along my slow slouch toward techno-Bethlehem so I would have a framework upon which to hang The Whole Rest Of My Life. Which starts now.

Or rather, then.

Back in 1989, to be exact. Freshman year. High school. The year I became a man. (And by man, I mean a scrawny, bird-like boy creature with a stupid haircut and a really real computer.)

Freshman year was rough. Not middle school rough, where the only thing I really had to worry about was whether or not I was wearing the right shoes or could at least pretend to like the right bands, but it was actually rough. As in shank a dude in the yard after chow rough.

Back then, my high school was separated into two distinct campuses: West Brook Senior High, which was for 10-12th graders, and Little Brook, which was for the plebeian interlopers in ninth grade, like me. It was completely walled in by a giant fence and iron gates, with armed prison guards stationed at every entrance. We called the warden a principal and tried to avoid making eye contact. It was a basically Shawshank, but without all the Morgan Freeman.

It was around this time that I realized I was an introvert. I'd always known I was a nerd, but now I was a nerd who didn't even like other nerds most of the time. Back in elementary school, I could throw a pre-LAN party for my birthday by putting a bunch of small television sets into our living room and hooking each one up to as many game consoles as possible, and nobody cared. But then The Hormones happened.

As my friends started to take an interest in things other than video games, fantasy books, or the Stars both Trek and Wars, I became more and more solitary. I began to look inward for fellowship, and I found my friends in books and movies and, most importantly, in games. My best friends started to have names like Shamino and Dupre, Bernard and Green Tentacle, Christopher Blair and Jeannette Devereaux, Guybrush Threepwood and Elaine Marley, etc... And I loved every minute of it. Even the horrible minutes. *Especially* the horrible minutes.

Get picked on at school for being a nerd?
Escape to games.

Get bullied for being too skinny or too fat or too whatever was funniest to the other kids that day?
Escape to games.

Openly mocked by your crush?
Escape to games.

Your best and only real friend moves across the country?
Escape to games.

I could go on, but you get the point. It didn't matter what was going on in my life, as long as I had my books and my games and my movies to rely on. But mostly, it was the games.

With games, I actually got to interact with "people" who respected and needed me, and we'd go on epic quests and save worlds together. One day, I'd be a crawling through an eerie dungeon while slaying evil creatures with my companions at my side, and I'd be a swashbuckling pirate with my own crew the next. A fierce warrior with loyal troops. A tunahead rescuing my girlfriend. An archaeologist searching for Atlantis with my research assistant. A Persian prince. A karate master. A travel agent in the land of the dead. I could figuratively become anyone I wanted, anywhere I wanted, any time I wanted. The worlds were mine.

Once I had the key, that is.

Which was technically an 8088 IBM clone with a 10-megabyte hard drive, EGA graphics, a 1200 baud modem, and a turbo button. But to me, it was the Narnia wardrobe and my personal Stargate to other worlds. I jumped into it as often as I could.

The first game I remember playing on that big, beautiful grey beast was Maniac Mansion. I can't be sure if it was *actually* the first thing I played, but it's the game that pulsates the hardest deep inside the squishy folds of my nostalgia hypothalamus, so let's go with it.

Maniac Mansion was a point-and-click adventure game and the place where cut-scenes came from. (It's true. The game's designer, Ron Gilbert, coined the term. Go on and Google it, if you don't believe me. I'll wait.)

I had no idea what I was doing while I was playing the thing, but I knew that I was loving it, whatever it was. I got to put a hamster in a microwave, break a crystal chandelier with the power of rock, and have an evil, sentient space rock arrested by the Meteor Police on live TV. Good times.

Maniac Mansion took my love of text adventures (most of which I played on my friend's "portable computer" because even text was almost too much for it to handle) and raised the stakes with graphics, a mouse pointer, and corny jokes.

I was hooked. In a bad way.

Seriously, I even watched the horrible Maniac Mansion TV show that nobody but me seems to remember. That's dedication, my friends.

That's dedication.

Interlude:
Yesterday's Future

The morning before the last flight of the Discovery ended, William Shatner woke up the crew with a re-working of the Star Trek opening monologue. The next day, the shuttle landed for the last time.

The end of the shuttle program heralded not just the end of an era in spaceflight, but rang out the last, tinny echoes of hope from a chorus that once sang of all that was bright and wondrous in this new world of technology and promise. Or, at least it was a new world. Back before we forgot that we live in the future.

I'm a child of the '80s. Not a pretender to the decade as so many wannabes who grew up in the '90s are, but a true, dyed-in-smurf-blue kid of the Reagan era. I grew up alongside computers, as PCs fought their way into the world, but before they'd taken over.

Back then, during the closing days of the Cold War, when Russia and Cuba could reasonably be expected to launch an assault on Colorado and Patrick Swayze, the air was different. Maybe it was because I was a kid, but it seemed like there was a bit of magic mixed in with the paranoia, and the future was an exciting new landscape of technology and innovation in which I couldn't wait to live.

Everything was new. Computers were new. Modems were new. Bulletin Board Systems held a tantalizing promise of digital community the world had never known. The future was everywhere. Lasers became commonplace, dizzying displays of light synced to the driving techno-chords of Moog synthesizers. Or Pink Floyd. Or both.

I built a robot in third grade. In sixth grade, I reproduced the hydroponics configuration of Walt Disney World's "The Land" with a motor, a hamster wheel, and a handful of tomato plants. I did everything I could to reach the future promised by the 1980s, a time where we collectively imagined we'd explore the frontiers of space and test the limits of the human mind. Technology would usher in a new era of humanity, ruled by science and reason and intellect. And flux capacitors.

But somewhere along the way, it all went wrong. I can't remember when it happened. I just know that it did.

The community of BBSs dissolved into the increasing chatter of FidoNET, which itself later fell to CompuServ, Prodigy and America On-Line, until the internet eventually ate them all. The sense of belonging to a digital family was washed away by the tidal surge of the Net and its ocean of limitless information. And noise.

Lasers, once a great symbol of science blending with the promise of art, a taste of lightsabers and ray guns, became nothing more than presentation tools for waterheaded MBAs to use during their torture sessions of PowerPoint and buzzwords. Now we use them to annoy our cats.

Computers stirred the imagination to touch the boundaries of the possible and push beyond them. Games rose up from text-only affairs to adventure and roleplaying games with crude graphics that provided more introspection than they did entertainment. They were a solitary activity, requiring a working knowledge of the arcane science of interrupt requests, input-output addresses and configuration files. Now, they're photorealistic, normal-mapped depictions of war and blood and brown. And sometimes they come in happy meals.

Where did our future go, exactly? All those years ago, I dreamed of a great world rising up decades later. But that was before the promise of innovation yielded to the demand for consumer products. I admit, my iPhone is amazing. I can watch movies on demand anywhere in the world (inasmuch as my carrier decides to provide coverage, that is). I can check my email, surf the web (does anyone even still say "surf" the web anymore) and buy any song I'll ever want with the touch of a button-shaped clump of pixels. It's amazing.

So why does it feel so cheap?

Maybe it's because I grew up. Maybe the hopes and dreams of youth are always dashed upon the jagged rocks of maturity. It happened to the hippies, when the flower-children of one decade became the yuppies of the next. I don't remember them, though. I was too busy playing with Star Wars toys and charting a course into the infinite unknowns of tomorrow to care about the mundane world of adults. The world I'm in now.

If it *is* meant to be this way - if the natural course of our lives is one of rising hope and crushing disappointment - then when the nose wheel of Discovery last touched the Earth, it was be the final step on a decades-long journey to nowhere. For all the convenience of our gadgets, the world isn't much different than it was back then. We just have more things that go bleep and bloop, and more ways to keep us up at night and away from all the things that ever really mattered.

I will always miss the days of my youth, when the future was an enormous playground of unending possibility. But what I miss more is the ability to hope and dream and wonder like I could back then. Whether it was because I was young and stupid, or if there really was any magic crackling through the atmosphere back when Woz was tinkering in his garage, it doesn't really matter. Whatever spark was there - or that I thought was there - is gone.

I can only hope my own kid feels some touch of it during these early days of his life, and that he's able to hold onto it longer than I have. And I hope that maybe, just maybe, I can get it back someday.

Chapter Seven

My first real computer brought me into the digital age before anyone even knew what the digital age was. It had a dot matrix printer and a word processor called PFS: First Choice, with a white-on-blue interface that made me feel like Doogie Howser whenever I'd write anything with it. I made random banners with Print Shop and used up reams of tractor-feed paper in the process. I dialed into BBS systems where I could finally go to the Files section and download things. Very, very slowly.

But mostly, I played games. Back then, PC gaming was all about the three staples: Adventure Games, RPGs, and Flight Simulators (along with a minor category I'll just call Random Whatevers). And 1989-1990 was a great time for Adventure Games.

After Maniac Mansion, I got my hands on Lucasfilm's next game (no, I didn't mean to say LucasArts; they weren't a thing yet), which was an odd little beast called Zak McKracken and the Alien Mindbenders. The game itself was pretty wacky, with a storyline involving tabloid journalism and aliens, but the weirdest thing is how I hardly remember it at all.

Maybe it's because the story went over my head, with all sorts of grown-up jokes that my virginal young mind was incapable of grasping. Maybe it was that I never got very far in it before the next game I obsessed over came out. Or maybe it was just all the dang mazes in the game. I really, really hate mazes.

For whatever reason, I don't have many Zak-related memories outside of Saved By The Bell and some horrific '80s nightmare commercial about someone called Zack The Lego Maniac that used to run incessantly during my after-school cartoons. (Yeah, I watched after-school cartoons in high school. And I watched before-school cartoons in high school because that's when G.I. Joe came on and screw you, don't judge me.)

But I do remember Lucasfilm's next game.

I remember it *hard*.

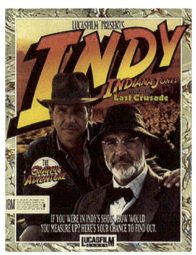

Indiana Jones and the Last Crusade was not only the last Indy movie (not counting Crystal Skull, which I'm not even going to get into right now), but it was also a couple of PC games. There was the Graphic Adventure, which is the one I'm going to talk about, and there was the Action Game, which was an abomination of both God and Nature that's best left forgotten to the mists of time. Seriously, it was awful. Forget what everyone says about Atari's E.T. game, which was actually not that bad for an Atari cartridge. There are plenty of better contenders for the title of The Worst Game Ever Made, and the Last Crusade Action Game is one of them.

The Graphic Adventure, on the other hand, was amazing. The box even shipped with a copy of Henry Jones' grail diary, complete with doodles and scribbles, and simulated coffee stains. And for a kid who both idolized George Lucas and wanted to grow up to be Indiana Jones, it was the perfect addition to an already fantastic game.

(*Sidenote*: Games often used to include little add-ins that were sometimes used as copy protection (the grail diary was vital to solving a puzzle in the game, for example), but were just as often included as part of immersing the player into the limited graphics of the game world. These little additions were called Feelies, and they started with the text adventure kings, Infocom. Their games, being all text, benefited greatly from these little touches, and Infocom had the most elaborate feelings around. From including the Wishbringer stone itself from Wishbringer, to a Don't Panic button and an official ball of fluff in Hitchhiker's Guide to the Galaxy, Infocom nailed the Feelies space, but they weren't the only ones who did it. Richard Garriott fought to include a cloth map of the world in every Ultima box, along with other trinkets like an Ankh, a coin, or a moonstone. I miss these things, as they were great collectibles before anyone had ever heard of charging triple the price for including similar items in so-called Collector's Editions of games.)

Several things happened to me after Indiana Jones and the Last Crusade was released, but the most pivotal was The

Algebra Teacher From Hell who was later quietly dismissed from the school district after vast discrepancies began appearing between students performing very well on standardized tests while failing his class miserably. (He was kind of a jerk.)

And, while I didn't get an F, I didn't get an A either, which was just as bad. I had, up until that year, been determined to attend the Air Force Academy, become a pilot, then transition into NASA where I could finally become an astronaut. But you don't get into the Air Force Academy with crappy grades in Algebra, and you certainly don't get in after your uncle - a retired Air Force Colonel - tells you that you have no chance of ever becoming a pilot because you're too tall and wear glasses, which is something that also happened that year. So yeah, with my dreams crushed by both a jerk teacher and a hope-murdering uncle, I floundered.

For the first time in my life, I didn't know what I wanted to be when I grew up. But then The Last Crusade happened, and I decided I could be Indiana Jones.

I was a weird kid.

Of course, it never happened. I did end up minoring in Anthropology in college though, so I got kind of close. But there's more to the Last Crusade than my dreams of tomb raiding. While I did want to be Indy - because, honestly, who wouldn't want to be Indy - I also thought I might enjoy making stuff up for a living, like George Lucas did. So I decided I'd also be a filmmaker.

Which also never happened.

Because life is an endless stream of trickling disappointments.

But anyway, back to the game.

I played the hell out of the graphic adventure. It hit all the right notes from the movies and then some, without ever deviating wildly from the source material, like so many licensed games tend to do. Also, the end sequence where Indy has to get through the trials to claim the grail was hilarious - but only if you died while doing it. I'm not going to spoil the joke though, so you'll just have to play it for yourself.

However, shortly after Indy and a handful of other games, something strange happened. I discovered that my amazing PC wasn't quite so amazing after all, because someone went and invented something called VGA and sound cards.

Which is when I took my first steps upon the Treadmill of Perpetual Torment us gamers call Upgrading Your PC. And it sucked.

I had to save all my pennies to buy a VGA adapter **and** a VGA monitor, which took way too long for my impatient teenage brain to endure. It eventually happened though, and the first game I remember playing was Prince of Persia. It had decent PC speaker support, so I didn't mind not having a sound card all that much, and the VGA graphics were beautiful to my impressionable young eyes.

I mostly sucked at the game and never managed to complete it, but it was a masterpiece of design that fell firmly into the Random Whatever category of PC gaming. It was an action game, but not exactly a sidescroller. It was a platformer, but not really. It had sword fighting, but only kind of. But on the whole, all the random pieces fit together to form a brilliant time-waster.

But it didn't hold me over for long, because all the pretty VGA versions of other games coming out also started shipping with sound card support, and I couldn't stand the fact that I was missing out on the AMAZING MIDI MUSIC and crackly, poorly-sampled digitized sounds of all these great games.

Fortunately, I didn't end up having to buy the sound card myself, because Santa left one under our Christmas tree in 1990, along with a copy of The Secret of Monkey Island.

And my world was forever changed.

Again.

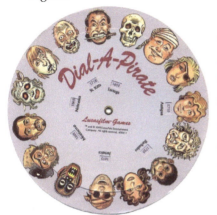

The Secret of Monkey Island was a revelation. From the opening notes of its brilliant soundtrack to its razor-sharp dialog and inventive puzzle design, it was everything I loved about gaming back then. I've always been a huge fan of the Pirates of the Caribbean ride at Disney World, and Monkey Island was that ride, given digital life. There had never been a greater surrogate for a player than Guybrush Threepwood, the bumbling pirate wannabe who had no idea what he was doing, and the jokes were just phenomenal.

(*Sidenote*: The Secret of Monkey Island would come back up way later in my life, after I learned that the girl I was seeing had also been a big fan of the game when she was younger. She'd played it with her brother, who was tragically killed in a car crash when the driver of an 18-wheeler fell asleep at the wheel. It was a special game to her for that reason, and it was a bond we shared from our childhoods. Naturally, when it came time to propose, I knew I had to somehow include it when I popped the question. So, with a little help from Ron Gilbert and the ScummC community, I modified the intro to Monkey Island 2 and used it to ask my wife to marry me. My nerdosity knows no limits.)

After Monkey Island came Ultima VI: The False Prophet, which was a game that dominated my time until I'd completed it, even if some of the design choices were a little crazy. Any time you had to interact with a container, which was all the time, you needed to spend approximately all the years of your life removing and replacing every single item inside it, one at a time. Also, the game used my fancy sound card for music but relied on the anemic *bloops* and *bleeps* of the PC speaker for sound effects, which really cheesed me off at the time. I still don't think I've forgiven it.

Of course, the most important thing about Ultima VI was that it brought me back to Ultima. After being unable to play the fifth game in the series when my Apple][clone lacked sufficient RAM, I hadn't set foot in Britannia since 1985. (Or maybe '86, depending on when I actually finished Ultima IV.) At any rate, I'd been away from my second home for far too long. And booting up Ultima VI for the first time really did feel like coming home.

Which leads me to a shocking confession: I'm one of the biggest Ultima fanboys on the planet, but I've never played Ultima V. Like, ever. It skipped me, so I skipped it. I really do need to go back and play it, but transitioning back into the world of Ten Million Keyboard Commands is hard when you're used to modern conveniences like actual user interfaces.

So there you have it. My secret shame. I never played what many people consider to be the best Ultima, simply because I couldn't run it at the time and nobody had bothered to tell me about the Upgrade Treadmill of Perpetual Torment back in 1988, so I didn't even realize I could've just bought more RAM.

Which was probably a good thing, in the end. The Apple][was on its way out anyway, and if I'd never been forced into getting an IBM clone back in '89, I might not have grown up to be the amazing nerd I am today.

So there's that.

Chapter Eight

When it came to developers back in the Golden Age of PC Gaming, there were The Big Three: Origin Systems, Lucasfilm/LucasArts Games, and Sierra On-Line. While I could easily start my discussion of The Big Three with LucasArts or Sierra, since I just touched on the subject of the Upgrade Treadmill of Perpetual Torment in the previous chapter, Origin seems the most logical choice.

You see, back before every game released required a new GPU or some other upgrade to run at its highest settings, Origin was already in the nasty habit of making gamers upgrade at least one part of their PCs in order to play whichever new game they put out. Whether it was upgrading to a VGA monitor for Ultima 6, or adding more RAM for Ultima 7, or upgrading all the things for any given Wing Commander game, no single company put more people on that damn treadmill back in the '90s than Origin.

Ultima VII, for example, (my personal favorite of the series, by the way, right next to Ultima IV) was every bit as much of a resource hog as it was a revolutionary roleplaying game. Because Richard Garriott is a madman who insisted on simulating the entire world of Britannia right down to the individual knives and forks on a peasant's dinner table, the game was an absolute beast on anything less than a really good 486 with a whole heaping helluva-lottaRAM to back it up. And even that wasn't enough, because the standard memory management of DOS couldn't even handle it. So naturally, Origin wrote their own system, which they very rightly named the Voodoo Memory Manager. And it was insane.

Without getting too much into nerdgasm technobabble, the standard DOS memory manager of the '90s could only access 640k of RAM by itself. Every other game on the planet that needed more memory at the time would use something called Protected Mode to access additional RAM, usually through an extender called DOS/4G. But not Origin. Oh, no. Since Austin, Texas is a place of lunatic genius, Garriott and company tapped into something called Unreal Mode because they were crazy people.

It caused all sorts of problems for players, which were usually solved by custom CONFIG.SYS and AUTOEXEC.BAT files or even separate boot floppies to keep their machines from loading standard memory management files like HIMEM and EMM386. And even then, with all of that sorted out, the game could still bring a beefy machine to its knees.

Until you upgraded.

Which we all did. Every time. Because it was totally worth it.

Origin dominated the "high end" side of game development, with what I guess would be considered the AAA blockbusters of the '90s, way before sneaky bastards in three-piece suits realized how much money there was in gaming and came in to ruin everything. And they did ruin everything, starting with Origin.

Back in the early '90s, Origin was creating worlds by pushing the envelope in ways no other developer had even thought about, which was great for gamers but also fatal for the company. They were operating at a time before the technology existed that they really needed (namely, CD-ROMs as the standard storage medium instead of floppy discs), and they were creating games on a scale that prohibited their continued self-publishing strategy. In short, you can't go from making games with a handful of people to giant teams without absorbing a huge loss to payroll - which alone, might be sustainable. But before CD-ROMs brought the increased data storage needed by the amazing, detailed games these big teams were creating, Origin was hit with a second gut punch of production costs. As in, physical production. When you're trying to cram enough data into a game that could easily fit on one CD-ROM, but that requires at least half a dozen high-density floppy discs, your manufacturing costs tend to shoot up. Way up.

And Origin couldn't sustain that. No company could. They couldn't create the games they wanted on the scale they wanted and still be profitable without help, which is when the Devil went down to Austin, looking for a soul to steal.

That devil was, of course, Electronic Arts, and the soul it stole was Origin's.

At first, EA was a saving grace. Origin increased its staff even more, bumped up game budgets, spent more time doing bigger and better things, and everything was peachy keen and nifty neato. Until it wasn't.

As any corporation staffed by an army of bean-counting suits is prone to do, EA eventually cracked down on Origin's growth, which is when things went pear-shaped. Origin slowly stopped being Dreamland and became just another corporate jungle. Teams fought for budgets over other teams, games siphoned resources from other games, and the general dog-eat-dog nature of office politics slowly poisoned the company.

The details of all of this have been well documented by people smarter than me, but the short of it is that Origin would've either died without EA, or it would've had to stop making the games it wanted to make and scale itself down into obscurity out of necessity. Because they were ahead of their time, Origin needed EA. But once time caught up to what Origin had already been doing for years, EA didn't need Origin.

So they killed it.

But even before all of that happened, the guys at Origin weren't stupid. They knew what signing that contract with the devil at the crossroads meant, even if they couldn't come right out and say it. But you can see it, even today. Because the enemy in Ultima VII: The Black Gate isn't the Fellowship or even the Guardian. It's Electronic Arts.

Back before EA started calling themselves EA with their "Challenge Everything" creepy kid-whisper campaign of nightmare splash screens, they were simply known as Electronic Arts. And their logo consisted of a cube, a sphere, and a tetrahedron.

Seems harmless enough, right?

If you've played Ultima VII, you might recognize these shapes from the Blackrock Generators the Fellowship built around Britannia to prepare the world for the coming of the Guardian through the Black Gate. The Guardian was an evil, malignant entity who descended upon peaceful Britannia to conquer and enslave its people. But he didn't go the way of brute force. Instead, he whispered into the ears of a few people. These people, in turn, created the Fellowship as a quasi-religious alternative to the Eight Virtues that the Avatar (the player) represented. At first, the people of Britannia flocked to the Fellowship, who were actually doing a lot of good in the world. Of course, it was all just window dressing to mask their true intent while they slowly and covertly positioned pieces on the chessboard for an eventual endgame of betrayal and tyranny.

Seeing any parallels yet?

The entire story of Ultima VII is the story of EA's acquisition of Origin. It was inevitable, unavoidable, and ultimately their downfall. But it was a necessary thing at the time, and the good it did for the company before things took a turn helped Origin create some of the most memorable and influential games in history.

Toward the end of his time at Origin and despite EA having had no faith in the project, Richard Garriott eventually created the first commercially successful MMORPG with Ultima Online. (So successful, in fact, that it basically killed Ultima IX...but that's another story for another chapter.) Wing Commander 3 brought the first Full Motion Video to gaming that didn't suck, with actual Hollywood talent and production values. (Let's just not mention the movie.) Wing Commander: Privateer was the X series before there was an X series. (Itself a new take on Elite, which had been long gone by then.) Bioforge was one of the first games to use pre-rendered 3D backgrounds with real-time 3D, texture-mapped polygonal characters, paving the way for the entire survival horror genre. (Think Resident Evil, but with aliens and robots.)

So yeah, Origin was Britannia and EA was the Fellowship, which also kind of means Richard Garriott was Lord British and Don Mattrick was the Guardian. If you're into metaphor and symbology or whatever.

That's just one theory, though. I have another.

My Absurd Alternative Guardian Theory

Some time ago, I decided that I was finally going to address my secret shame of never having actually played Ultima V by actually playing Ultima V. I downloaded a copy off my GOG.com game shelf, then snagged the Combined Bonus Pack of manuals and artwork, reference cards, etc... To bring myself up to speed on everything that had been going on in Britannia up to that point, and to gently massage my nostalgia gland, I opened up The Book of Lore that shipped with the game.

Then, I found this on page 23:

Look at that face. JUST LOOK AT IT.

Tell me that isn't the Guardian. Just look at the face of this nameless blacksmith and try telling me he's not the evil red muppet man from Ultima VII. You can't do it!

Because he IS the Guardian. Or, at least he will be. Eventually.

See, I have an alternative theory about the Guardian's origins that have nothing at all to do with either Origin or Electronic Arts. My theory takes place entirely within the established fiction of Ultima's canonical storyline. And it goes a little something like this...

The unnamed blacksmith pictured in Ultima V's Book of Lore is actually Naughty Nomaan, from the town of Jhelom. In Ultima V, he wasn't much more than a generic vendor without much to say. But by Ultima VI, Nomaan had become a serious man of virtue by winning the Rune of Valor in a contest held by the town's mayor, Zellivan.

Presumably uplifted by his victory, Nomaan tried his best to shed his "Naughty" moniker. Holding the Rune of Valor, representing one of the Eight Virtues, put Nomaan a little closer to the Avatar, who was himself the embodiment of those Virtues. Unfortunately, Nomaan lost the rune after he accidentally dropped it in the Sword and Keg tavern, where it was quickly snatched by a rat and carted off into the walls.

When the Avatar comes plodding into Jhelom in Ultima VI (notice how similar his portrait from Ultima VI is to The Guardian's face in Ultima VII: same square jaw, same straight horizontal line of a mouth, etc…), Nomaan is naturally excited to meet this man he not only admires, but also with whom he shares what he feels is a common bond through their valorous deeds. He confides to the Avatar that he dropped the rune and tells him about the rat, confident that the physical embodiment of the Eight Virtues will help him reclaim it.

Of course, that never happens. The Avatar just uses Nomaan's information to locate the Rune and keep it for himself, since he needs it to, like, save the world and stuff by using it at the Shrine of Valor along with the Mantra of Valor because of the RPG Law Of Threes. (Also, he can't get the rune without the help of Sherry the talking mouse in Lord British's castle, who was a character inspired by a former girlfriend of Garriott's, but that's too much subtext for me to parse on an empty stomach, so we'll just ignore it for now.)

Betrayed by the Avatar, Nomaan reverts back to his naughty ways and quickly falls in with the wrong crowd, who probably have something to do with one of Mondain's Gem of Immortality fragments or maybe Minax's evil something or other because those two really screwed things up for everyone back in the '80s, but whatever. The specifics have been lost to time, with the end result being that Nomaan's hatred of the Avatar eventually becomes so great and eats at him for so long that he transforms into the creature known as The Guardian by Ultima VII.

Need more proof? Fine. Just check out this official tarot card from Ultima IX, depicting the virtue of Valor. Remember that Naughty Nooman lived in Jhelom, the town of Valor and temporarily had possession of the Rune of Valor, so Valor is pretty much his whole thing. Now look at the tarot card. Why is a giant red face on it?

BECAUSE HE'S THE GUARDIAN, THAT'S WHY!

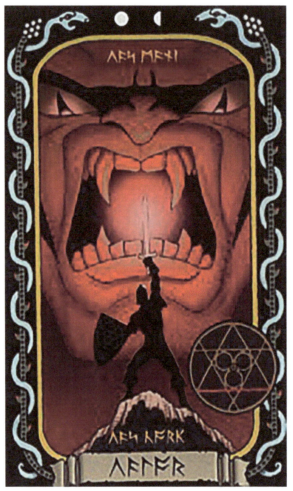

I rest my case.

Chapter Nine

I love Adventure Games. Always have, always will. This chapter isn't about adventure games, though. It's about the two companies that defined the genre, and how different from one another they truly were. This all goes a little sideways toward the end, by the way. You might need a tissue.

You have been warned.

All of my gaming memories are adventure gaming memories. Or something like that, anyway. Okay, maybe not all of them, but most of them. Especially the oldest ones. The best ones. (I even consider the Ultima series to be more on the Adventure side of the gaming spectrum than the Roleplaying side. Which is a good thing, I promise.)

As I mentioned way back in Chapter Whatever, Maniac Mansion was the first game I remember playing on my first IBM-compatible PC, which was basically just a nameless, generic grey box, but I loved it all the same. After Maniac Mansion, most of the games I remember are adventure games and RPGs, with the occasional flight sim or RTS thrown in for good measure because I believe it's important to be well-rounded and stuff.

Anyway, way back in the heyday of the point and click adventure, there were two companies synonymous with quality: LucasArts and Sierra. Except that Sierra sucked and only losers liked their games!

Of course, that wasn't remotely true. But it was considered The Great Rivalry back in the day, and you had to choose a side. Or at least pretend to choose a side, which is all most people did. I played all the games from both companies, but my heart always belonged to LucasArts. (Or Lucasfilm, before it got all fancy and started putting extra capital letters in its name.)

After Maniac Mansion, the first game I truly remember loving was Indiana Jones and the Last Crusade - but I already talked about that in Chapter Seven, so we'll move on to The Secret of Monkey Island. Except I've already talked about that one, too. Crap. Maybe all of my gaming memories really *are* adventure gaming memories.

It's true, though. I deeply, deeply loved LucasArts as a company. Like, probably more than is legal. Don't believe me? Just check out my love letter to them after this chapter. You'll get the diabetes.

I could spend this whole chapter waxing nostalgic for my favorite LucasArts adventure games, but there's not much left of that poor dead horse I keep beating on, so I'll skip straight to Sierra.

Or rather, what made Sierra adventure games different from LucasArts adventure games.

Because they really were different.

First, they were kinda racist as all get out. Seriously, go back and play a Police Quest or two and tell me how many minorities obviously didn't work at Sierra back in the '90s. I guess it shouldn't be too shocking though, seeing as how they eventually crawled into bed with Daryl Gates. But it was always there, from the stereotypes of Leisure Suit Larry to the stereotypes of King's Quest, Quest for Glory, Gabriel Knight, and nearly every other game they ever made. Sierra made games for well-off white people living in the "good" end of town, which considering how much those nameless grey boxes we called PCs cost back then, might not have really been that far off the mark. They did rise to prominence during Reaganomics, after all.

Of course, it was a different time, I guess. That excuse gets used a lot. It was also more likely less-intentioned racism so much as it was just the comfy casual racism of the '80s and '90s suburbs. I mean, black people just talked like that, right? Hispanic people always sound like Speedy Gonzales, don't they? Gay dudes are always aggressively feminine and sassy, aren't they?

(The answer to all of those rhetorical questions is obviously no, but I felt like I should point out the sarcasm before someone starts a hashtag on Twitter.)

It was dinner table bigotry. And it permeated almost everything Sierra did, which always bothered me, even before I really understood it.

Second, they weren't funny. Sure, they had a couple of comedy series like Space Quest and Larry, but by and large, the Sierra games told "serious" stories by way of ridiculously one-dimensional characters and lots and lots of really awful puns. Or really great puns, I guess. It probably depends on your tolerance for puns. I have none.

Third, they didn't keep up with technology. Sure, they cranked out more games than LucasArts, but their over-reliance on their outdated AGI and SCI game engines really showed when put next to a LucasArts game. While the latter was pushing the envelope of what was possible with detailed animations and visually expressive characters, Sierra was content to stay with the same blobby, amorphous faces of its barely animated characters. Although, to be fair, they relied on character portraits during conversations for expressiveness. So there was that. It's something.

Fourth, they killed you. A lot. And often in really stupid, unpredictable ways that some game designer thought was funny because they could make a pun out of it. Honestly, if you've never played an old Sierra game, you just don't understand how much those daffy bastards loved their puns. In contrast, LucasArts games never killed you. And if they did, it was entirely foreseeable and preventable and come on, just get Guybrush out of the water before he drowns, okay?

Along the same lines, Sierra games were usually horribly broken, design-wise. In theory, this added to the challenge of completing a game, but in practice, it just led to frustration and anger. See, in most Sierra games, there was no plot funneling. You could easily pass through a one-way section of the game with no way to return, only to find out hours, days, weeks, or months later (this was during the dark ages before god invented internet walkthroughs) that you needed to do something or talk to someone or pick something up way back at the start of the game that you wouldn't ever need until the end of the game. And you'd be screwed. Restore/Restart/Quit!

Fifth, they were still fun. Even if they had no real right to be, judging from all the griping I've just been doing about them, they were still fun games. Being a space janitor was fun. Being a frontier pharmacist was fun. Getting RPG peanut butter in your adventure game chocolate in the Quest for Glory series was fun. Yeah, the games were a little racist and had faceless characters who spouted off cringe-worthy dialog between endless nonsensical death sequences, but they were still a good time. Somehow.

Now, take every point I just made, flip it around, and shoot it back at LucasArts, and you have the basic idea of what BBS and Usenet flame wars were like back in the late '80s, through the mid-'90s. Sierra fans liked the challenge of dying. They liked getting to the end of a game, only to realize they couldn't complete the story because they forgot to pick up the snozberries hidden in the back of a random desk drawer in the third screen. They liked the art style. They dug the lack of animation. Everything LucasArts did was too slickly produced, too overly polished. Too mainstream and dumbed down for the masses.

Sierra fans were hipsters before hipsters were cool.

One thing I will always remember Sierra doing that LucasArts never (to my knowledge) did, is an odd little thing. It's kind of stupid, actually. But that's how memories work. The weird things tend to stick to the mental Velcro in your braincase, while everything else just sorts of slides off like a fried egg on a Teflon pan.

What I remember most are the Christmas cards. Or one, really. Sierra used to put out these little holiday greetings every year, but the one from 1992 has stuck with me the longest. And I have no idea why.

I was a senior in high school that year, so maybe the pivotal moment of graduation gave it more meaning? Somehow, I doubt it. Maybe I was going through some stuff, and the card just hit at the right time to get me all sentimental or something. Who knows?

Well, now that I think about it, maybe I do. And it had nothing to do with 1992, except that was the year they released it, and it was the year I showed it to my grandmother. She loved Christmas and really got a kick out of the little digital card. The snow, the music, the cheery candle and the fireplace. The deer. It was just a warm little fuzzy of the holiday season, and she really dug it. So I'd show it to her every year after that, and every year she would enjoy it like she was seeing it for the first time.

I was incredibly close to my grandmother.

She died shortly before her birthday nine years later. I only got to show her that stupid Christmas card nine times - if that, since I'm sure I missed a year or two while being Young And Stupid - but I still watch it every year and think of her. I mix that warm holiday fuzzy with the bitter melancholy of age, and I miss her. And the '90s. And the '80s. And all the years of my life that are gone, along with all the people who have left with them.

Which pretty much defines nostalgia, I guess.

And why we need it.

Always.

Dang. Now I need a hug.

Ugh. I'm trying my best to keep these chapters at least a little bit funny, but this one took a turn. Sorry about that. The next one will have more fart jokes or something. I promise.

Interlude:
Remembering LucasArts

The closing of LucasArts in 2013 affected me far more than it should have. After all, it was just a game studio, and one that hadn't produced anything of note in years before it shut down. Still, the impact that Lucasfilm Games (later to become LucasArts) had on me in my formative years is not something I can easily dismiss. In fact, it even touched my grown-up years, when Monkey Island became something of a shared bond between me and my wife. Heck, I even used Monkey Island 2 to propose to her. (More on that in Chapter Seven, if you're skipping around.)

But let's back up from my geek proposal and wind the clock back to 1987. Or hop in a Chron-O-John. Whichever you prefer.

I was in seventh grade, a geek in '80s neon and Coca-Cola shirts with a Swatch on my wrist and Converse on my feet. And in my bedroom, I had one of the approximately ten gigazillion Apple clones floating around at the time. I spent my free time alternating between playing games and hopping on Bulletin Board Systems (BBS) with my fancy 300 baud modem.

Lucasfilm Games had been around for a few years at that point, but the only game I'd ever played that was remotely connected to them was The Empire Strikes Back on my Atari 2600. The entire game consisted of taking down chunky AT-AT shaped rectangles with minus signs fired from your blocky Snowspeeder. It was fun, but not exactly enthralling. But in 1987, Lucasfilm released a game that would change everything.

Of course, I had to wait until Christmas of the next year before I finally got an 8088 IBM clone, which is when I discovered Maniac Mansion. Created by Ron Gilbert - the man who I credit as having built LucasArts - it was one of the first graphic adventures I'd ever played. Sure, I'd toyed around with a couple of King's Quest games on the Apple][, and I'd spent many, many hours questing around Britannia (well, Sosaria and Earth in different time periods, but eventually Britannia) in the Ultima series, but I'd never experienced anything like Maniac Mansion. It was point-and-click. You chose from multiple characters to play through the story with three of them. And everyone always picked Bernard. (Because nerds stick together.)

After that, I was hooked. It didn't hurt that I basically idolized George Lucas at the time, either. I played everything from Lucasfilm in those early years. And I do mean everything. I considered it my duty to support the studio because it was a way to support Lucas himself - as if he needed the steady influx of my allowance. I tangled with alien mindbenders in Zak McKracken. I fought Nazi pilots in Battlehawks 1942, and later in Their Finest Hour and Secret Weapons of the Luftwaffe. I built action figures in Night Shift, and I became an expert hacker years before Bioshock by playing Pipe Dream. I willingly bought and made myself play the Indiana Jones and the Last Crusade action game...and it was pretty awful. I even watched the brief run of the Maniac Mansion television series, which was its own kind of awful. But in a good way. Sort of.

The history of Lucasfilm Games is the history of my adolescence. I waited all year to get a Sound Blaster for Christmas, specifically because of The Secret Of Monkey Island's soundtrack. I annoyed the crap out of my local WaldenSoftware with endless phone calls when they *still* didn't have the talkie version of Day Of The Tentacle, even though I knew it was out. And when I finally got it (in the triangle box, which I kept for years, but eventually lost in a hurricane), I was enraged that they didn't bother to buffer the sound effects for my single-speed CD-ROM drive. Each time purple tentacle hopped, the game stuttered as the pathetic drive I'd spent all my money on struggled to keep up. So I saved up again and bought a double-speed drive, and all was right with the world.

And that's how it went, for years. It's safe to say I was a dedicated fan. I remember being sad when Ron Gilbert left to start Humongous Entertainment. I was crushed when Tim Schafer left after Grim Fandango. And my heart broke when I read the news that Disney had shut down LucasArts altogether.

So it's with equal parts nostalgia and melancholy that I write this now. So many memories are flooding back that I doubt I can cram them all in, but one that sticks out the most was from the Indiana Jones and the Last Crusade graphic adventure (**not** the action game...this is an important point). I have a very distinct memory of sitting in my room at my computer and loading the game. The Lucasfilm logo came up and did a little sparkly thing as the Indiana Jones theme began to play. I was a freshman in high school at the time, and I decided right then that I would work for Lucasfilm one day, either on games or on movies. It didn't matter. I just wanted to be part of that world and work with the people in it.

But I never did.

I did eventually write an impassioned letter to LucasArts at one point, letting them know that I was coming to work for them as soon as I got out of high school. I'm not sure what I said exactly, but I'm fairly certain it was awful. And pretentious. And probably unintentionally hilarious.

To my surprise, I actually got a reply. And it wasn't a form letter, either. It was, basically, the nicest brush-off letter anyone has ever written. I don't remember what it said, but I do remember that it was kind and reassuring and supportive. And I remember who wrote it, and I still follow her (on Twitter, that is; I'm not a stalker) to this day. Her name was Khris Brown, and she went on to become a fantastic voice director, but who was in Product Support at the time. I remember her letter not only because it was so kind, but because she spelled her name as oddly as I spell mine. It was another connection to this world I so desperately wanted to be a part of. And it didn't feel like a blow-off letter, either. My pleas weren't ignored as I'm sure they would've been had I written to any other company. It was encouraging and thoughtful and upbeat, and even a little inspiring. I'll never forget it.

I never did go to work at Lucasfilm, though. And now I never will. Its era has passed, the sale to Disney the final nail in its coffin. I doubt its magic will ever be reproduced, although companies like Double Fine give me hope, along with non-publishing publishers like Kickstarter helping to fund projects that would otherwise never see the light of day. The magic of the Lucasfilm days may never again come together under one roof, but the sparks are still out there. Ron Gilbert is still making games. Tim Schafer is still making games. Other veterans of the studio are still making games. There's still hope, but part of the wonder is gone now. Even though LucasArts hadn't really made a good game in years, as long as they were around, there was still hope that they could somehow get the magic back. And now that hope is lost.

I'll always regret never having had a chance to work in the environment that produced such amazing games and encouraged such zany creativity. My own career path has meandered from working in IT to becoming a web designer, to a brief stint as a journalist and back around again to technology where I spent some time working for the Black Mesa/Aperture Science/Umbrella Corporation of the real world before settling into editing and writing for a living. It's a good gig and I enjoy the work, but if I had a chance to drop everything to go sweep the floors at Double Fine just so I could occasionally have coffee with Tim Schafer, I'd probably do it. And I hate coffee.

Lucasfilm / LucasArts
1982 - 2013

And that's it. So long, LucasArts. I was there with you when you were Lucasfilm Games, and I was there with you when you changed your name. And I'll always be with you. Like the Force, only less mystical. Or maybe more. Like I said, it was a magical place and the world won't soon see anything like it again.

Chapter Ten

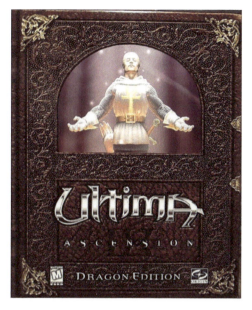

You've probably noticed by now that most of these chapters are dominated by Origin, LucasArts, and Sierra. If you're looking for a more comprehensive history of gaming, flip over to the Bonus Feature toward the end of the book. My Top 10 PC Games of All the Years list should satisfy whatever itch you're having for other games made by other studios. But for now, back to Origin. Also, I'm jumping ahead in time here a little bit for this chapter because I can't spend so much time on the Ultima series in this book and not touch on Ultima IX.

Every now and then, a game comes along that's so amazing, so inspiring, so transformative that it changes everything. Ultima IX was not one of those games. Except that it kinda was.

You can catch up on the Origin story of this chapter by reading Chapter Eight, or you can skip it and just jump straight into the deep end with me as I bring you my "review" of Ultima 9. It's only a couple decades late. No big deal.

People **hate** this game, and I've never understood why. It's not a bad game, and it's definitely nowhere near the "worst RPG ever" as some have described it. Nor is it a betrayal, as others have proclaimed it to be. It's just what it is: a good game wrapped in impossible expectations, with a side of french fried bad timing.

First up, the hate. It's actually been building over the years, like an angry little snowball rolling down the side of a mountain in a Saturday morning cartoon. However, contrary to what people want to believe *now*, it wasn't actually hated *then*. Not really. Sure, it wasn't given glowing reviews, but it wasn't universally loathed in the legendary way it has become over the years. At the time, it received, at worst, a lukewarm reaction.

The biggest gripe fans had way back in 1999 when the game came out had to do with performance and compatibility issues more than anything to do with the game itself. People didn't start ripping apart the plot and yelling about things like, "What's a paladin?" until much later, after YouTube happened and taking giant dumps on other people's hard work became a subscriber-fetching trend.

So let's roll the clocks back to November 24, 1999 - which is the day Wikipedia tells me Ultima IX came out because I'm too old and senile to remember it without looking. But whatever day it came out is the day that I had it. And the Dragon Edition, no less. I still have my tarot cards to prove it!

Imagine me driving back to my apartment, giddy with excitement to play the latest installment of a game series that meant a lot to me, growing up. It's something I played with my dad, and it forms some of my earliest memories. We bonded over stopping Minax. We learned about each other by discussing Ultima IV. We yelled in solidarity when we played Ultima VII and just wanted EVERYBODY TO SIT THE HELL DOWN ALREADY in the damn wagon. It was a thing the two of us shared that kept me from ever entering that horrible father-hating teenage rebellion stage, and I will always - *always* - be thankful for that.

But anyway, it's not 1985, so enough with my Dad-memories. It's 1999, and I've just arrived home and installed the game. I load it up and...it probably crashed. Because that's what Ultima IX did when it was released. It crashed a lot. But so did every Origin game, which people tend to forget. Games from Origin were always demanding, always punishing to older systems, and always, always buggy. But this was 1999, and the internet had happened, which made getting patches a whole lot faster and easier than the BBS days, and the Ultima IX team was quick with early patching.

I didn't have a lot of the same problems other people had with the game, because I had a 3DFX card in my system. However, a lot of people didn't, at this point. Ultima IX had the misfortune of coming out during the awkward transition period between Glide and Direct3D. In the early days of 3D PC gaming, 3DFX was king, and *everything* used Glide, its proprietary API. OpenGL and Direct 3D cards weren't very big in those early days, and the ones that did exist were usually slow and clumsy things when compared with the screaming speed of dual Voodoo 2s.

But Ultima IX hit when things were beginning to change after Nvidia came on the scene with their TNT line of graphics cards. They were getting popular, and Origin didn't see it coming. Or, if they did, they didn't have time to adjust.

But before that, the very first iteration of Ultima IX didn't even take 3DFX cards into account, as it was entirely software-rendered. But once the rise of graphics accelerators happened, they knew that they had to get on board, otherwise their game would be behind the curve. So they scrapped the engine and wrote a new one - and, well, this story has been famously told and retold to the point that most every gamer knows what happened by heart.

In short: Electronic Arts moved the Ultima IX development team to Ultima Online, then back to Ultima IX when it was done, after which they slapped it with a restrictive budget and an impossible deadline. And the rest is history.

Or is it?

One commonly held belief is that Ultima IX was always intended to be the last Ultima, at least by the time development started on the third and final iteration of the game. It turns out, though, that's not entirely true.

When I asked Richard Garriott about this, he had this to say:

"That was never intended to be the last Ultima! It was only the end of the trilogy of trilogies. Ultima ended with my departure."

This is an important point to consider when remembering Ultima IX, because the one thing a lot of people seem to have developed a problem with (over time) is its story. Specifically, with how it basically saddles the Avatar with amnesia regarding the events of the previous games, along with breaking series canon in numerous ways. But more on that in a minute. First, we need to get back to me playing the game back in good old 1999.

I loved it. I installed the game, I patched the game, I tweaked my machine until it ran the game as smoothly as it was ever going to, and I played the game. AND I LOVED IT.

Seeing Britannia come to life in 3D for the first time (outside of the Underworld games) was a revelation. Sure, sacrifices had to be made to render the world in all three of the glorious dimensions, but I didn't mind that Britain was suddenly a tiny hamlet, or that you could see the skybox inside Lord British's throne room because the view distance was so short. I was a lifelong gamer. I understood the nature of compromise when it came getting available technology to do what you wanted it to do.

And those graphics? They hold up. Even today, they're still pretty to look at, and more detailed than anything else out there at the time. Britannia wasn't just a bunch of polygons on a tiny world map. It was alive with fluttering birds and skittering insects. There were trees and foliage. Things in caves went drip. It was entirely immersive, despite the limitations of the engine.

What else was doing what Ultima IX did in 1999? Nothing, that's what.

Sure, Quake hit in '96, and it was fast and looked great, but it wasn't a very richly detailed world. Unreal looked even better than Quake - and it even had some life in it, with waterfalls and insects buzzing around, but it was still a nailed-down shooter. The geometry was a playset to run around in, not a world to be explored.

But Ultima IX was filled with little details like the sound of footfalls being attached to world textures so that when you ran over sand, it sounded like sand, and when you ran over wood or stone, it sounded like wood or stone. That was new back then. *People forget.*

There were also no loading screens. None. Once you were in the world, you stayed in the world. You didn't open a door to watch a loading screen hit you with a separate Tavern Instance. You just opened the door and walked in. Same with dungeons. An open world with no loading screens. Nothing else was doing that in 1999. *People forget.*

And about those dungeons: they were great! Even the annoying ones (I'm looking at you, Hythloth) were detailed and intricate and fun. The closest comparison one could make with the complexity of Ultima IX's dungeons would be along the lines of the Tomb Raider series. Of course, the Avatar wasn't as agile as Lara Croft, but the puzzles, the length, the immersion was all there - along with the open world above ground, and the NPCs, and the dialog trees, and the overall plot, and the multiple locations. Everything. In nineteen freaking ninety-nine.

PEOPLE FORGET.

Also released in 1999, EverQuest was the closest anything came to doing what Ultima 9 did. Look at that ground texture. JUST LOOK AT IT.

Once the technical hurdles had been overcome with the final patches from Origin, people who wanted to dislike the game - or who were still feeling burned by its unfinished nature at release - moved on from performance issues to gameplay and story problems. Which is where the modern day critics come in.

Most of the their complaints stem from the story, and from a sense of betrayal at the hands of an uncaring developer. Or, rather, publisher. Most people blame Electronic Arts.

And so do I. So does everyone. Ultima IX without Electronic Arts would've undoubtedly been one of those amazing games I mentioned at the beginning of this chapter, just like every Ultima before VIII was one of those amazing games that changed everything. Nobody likes EA. I get that. We all get that.

But...it's not entirely EA's fault.

Nor is anyone to blame for things that aren't really problems, to begin with.

Yes, Ultima IX severely retconned the previous fiction.

Yes, Ultima IX basically gave the Avatar amnesia.

Yes, Ultima IX catered more to new players than it did to returning players.

AND NONE OF THIS WAS BAD.

The landscape of gaming was changing dramatically in 1999. Not only had 3D taken a firm hold of the future, but the entire industry was changing. The era of the "hardcore" gamer was ending, and gaming was transitioning into something more mainstream. Naturally, the hardcore gamers resented this - just look at the hate something like Deus Ex 2 received from complaints that it was "dumbed down" and "console-ified" to see it.

The hardcore market was also shrinking. People tend to get less "hardcore" about anything as they get older and other demands for their time start taking priority over gaming. Careers, family, children, mortgages, etc... Things add up, and people start leaving the hobby, or at least abandoning the "hardcore" games for titles that are easier to slip into and back out of again after the baby monitor goes off and you've got to get a crying infant back to sleep. It happens.

This sword was especially sharp for something like Ultima, which not only needed to attract new players, but somehow still please the returning ones. Which brings me around to what I said a few minutes ago: that Ultima IX was never intended to be the last Ultima.

It's a popular sentiment now, that EA always knew Ultima IX was going to be the last single-player game in the series. It's become accepted as just how it was, and I think that idea is partly behind some of the hardcore gamers' hate for the game. Why cater to new players, after all, if you're ending the series? Why "dumb down" the game for the fans, just so you can attract new players to a series that won't have another installment?

And I totally get that. I'd probably be angry, too, if that were the case. But Ultima IX was not always meant to be the end to the series - just the final installment of the third trilogy. The series didn't end until Richard Garriott left Origin, regardless of what EA might've had in mind.

So, yes. At the time it was being developed, Ultima IX had to adapt to the new gaming landscape. It had to bring in new players, and it had to go easy on returning players who might not have memorized every last little detail and event that happened over the course of a series that had been running continuously for the past EIGHTEEN YEARS.

A lot of Ultima fans in 1999 who had come on board with Ultima VI or VII probably weren't even alive when Ultima 1 came out. Heck, even a 15-year-old kid loading up Ultima IX for the first time would've only been 7 or 8 years old when the start of the Guardian trilogy, Ultima VII, was released. How much detail could you remember at 15 from when you were only 7? Probably not very much.

Which is why Ultima IX needed to do something for everyone who wasn't a member of the hardcore superfans club. In an era before the concept of rebooting a franchise ever occurred to anyone, Ultima IX had to straddle the line between introduction and continuation, in a sort of quasi-reboot dance that a lot of players have since come to look back on with disdain.

Which, I think, is faulting the game for something beyond its control. Sure, it wasn't handled as adeptly as we've come to expect from more recent attempts at doing the same thing (the Marvel cinematic universe comes to mind), but it was charting new territory. Again.

Because that's what Ultima did. With every new entry in the series, it did something new. Most of the time, it worked. Ultima IV was a bombshell that showed you could have an engaging RPG without a Slay The Foozle plot. Ultimas V and VI heaped pounds of ambiguity onto the virtuous narrative and gave the series more and more nuance. Ultima VII poked the religion bear with a stick. And each new game featured new tech. Each and every one.

Other times - *cough* Ultima VIII *cough* - they didn't quite hit the mark. But for every one Ultima VIII (or, I admit, the horribly misguided and woefully executed romance subplot of Ultima IX), I can show you 7.5 other Ultima games that nailed it, along with two others that took the adventure to the Underworld and did things no one had ever seen before.

That's a pretty good track record, and Ultima IX is somewhere closer to the Good side of that number line than the Bad side. Yes, it's closer to Ultima VIII, but only by way of it not being Ultima IV or VII. It's less good by comparison, but it is in no way bad.

In fact, it's even improved with age. The graphics really do hold up, and the GOG.com version is stable, with higher frame rates, resolutions, and view distances than were ever possible back in 1999. You should really check it out.

I know I've been having fun with it. I think you will, too.

So, go on.

Try it.

All the cool kids are playing Ultima IX, after all.

Don't you want to be cool, too?

This was my childhood.

Chapter Eleven

Let's hit pause on the video games for a minute to talk about books. Specifically, I want to talk about the books that made me a nerd, or maybe they're the books I read because I was already a nerd. I don't know; it's a chicken and egg type of situation. At any rate, I became an avid reader somewhere along the line, which was looked down upon in the Deep South of the 1980s...just like every other aspect of nerd culture, really.

Not that nerd culture was even a thing back then, of course. In the '80s, there were no nerdy titans of industry, geek subculture hadn't come anywhere near breaking into the mainstream, and everything about being a nerd was confusing and foreign to everyone who wasn't a nerd. We were weirdos and freaks, and were the natural prey of Normies for decades before enough of us got together and turned the tables on society. Things are pretty sweet for us these days, but back then? Not so much.

I'd always liked reading as a kid, but I didn't discover the true joy of the hobby until I was around 10-years-old and found myself wandering around Waldenbooks one random day at the mall. Being a fan of the Ultima games and RPGs in general, I was already into knights and dragons and all things fantasy, so it was pretty common to find me rummaging through the Sci-Fi section of bookstores - which might not make much sense, but Fantasy wouldn't be recognized as a popular genre until later, so they always just shelved the Fantasy books in the Sci-Fi section - which is something they still do, except at least they call it "Sci-Fi & Fantasy" now. So there's that.

When I was younger, I normally stuck to books and series I knew, which mostly included Encyclopedia Brown and Choose-Your-Own-Adventures. I loved Encyclopedia Brown right up until the stories started getting stupid. I remember the last one I read because it so enraged me that I swore off the series forever, right then and there. The guilty guy ended up being a character that was only ever half-mentioned in the story, and the assumptions necessary to conclude that he was the bad guy were so ridiculous that I nearly lost all faith in deductive logic. Seriously, that last book really pissed me off. I'm still upset about it. I can hold a grudge, y'all.

As far as Choose-Your-Own-Adventures, I had stacks and stacks of these books, from the normal white-and-red ones in the main product line to knock-offs that jumped on the bandwagon and started putting out licensed CYOAs with characters I loved, like Indiana Freaking Jones. Then, there were the Choose-You-Own-Adventure and RPG hybrid books like Lone Wolf, which mixed the two genres in interesting ways that I'm still impressed a book was able to pull together. To this day, I don't understand how a book was able to know how many hit points I had left. HOW?!

These were just kid books, though. It wasn't until that one day in that one Waldenbooks that I would find that one special book that would set me on a course I'd follow for the rest of my life. At first, it looked just like any other Fantasy book: the yellow spine of the paperback was just sitting in a line with all the other books, but something about the title caught my eye.

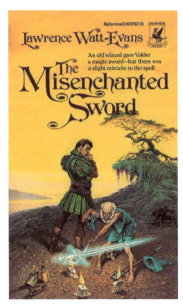

I reached out my little 10-year-old hand and pulled The Misenchanted Sword by Lawrence Watt-Evans from the shelf to examine the cover. It had everything.

Sword: **Check**

Sorcery: **Check**

Knight: **Check**

Wizard: **Check**

Flowery "Medieval" Font: **Check**

"An old wizard gave Valder a magic sword - but there was a slight mistake in the spell."

That was all I needed. Going against all the advice I'd ever heard growing up, I judged the book by its cover, then immediately went to the cash register and bought it with my lawn-mowing money. I started reading it before we'd even left the mall parking lot, and made myself sick somewhere between the Burger King and our driveway because I never could read in the car.

I don't know what it was about that book that hit me so hard, but I'm pretty sure it had something to do with it being the perfect blend of cliché and subversion, drama and comedy, playing it straight and going satirical. It was the first exposure I had to the idea that you could actually play around with genre conventions and twist them here and there to create something new, yet familiar. It showed me that you could have comedy in a serious story, and that even the most earnest tale could somehow satirize its genre while still being a perfect example of it.

If you've never read it, you should give it a shot. I read through it every few years, and it holds up every bit as well today as it did when I was 10-years-old. But The Misenchanted Sword was only the beginning.

The next book I'd pick up at that same Waldenbooks changed me forever. I'd gone back to the store to see if Lawrence Watt-Evans had anything else I could read, and I went right back to the Sci-Fi section to start browsing by author...but got lost somewhere around the middle of the alphabet. In the Ps, specifically.

Terry Pratchett.

The first Pratchett book I ever bought was Reaper Man, which taught me everything I ever needed to know about satire...until the next Pratchett book showed me that I still had a lot to learn. Every "next Pratchett book" did that, and I devoured them all. I was still reading Lawrence Watt-Evans, and I picked up Douglas Adams somewhere along the way, but nobody sang to me quite like Pratchett. He taught me that *what* you write isn't nearly as important as *how* you write it. The plot of your average Discworld book is all over the place, but the individual moments that make up each one are focused and refined to such a degree that it comes back looking like it took no effort at all. Pratchett showed me how to turn a

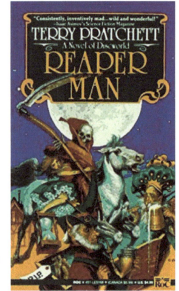

phrase, even if I never quite learned how to do it at his level. And I probably never will.

He also taught me that the craft of writing is more important than the story each sentence is building. Plot doesn't matter very much, not really. All the good plots have already been taken, so it's up to the writer to make them interesting again. We've all read about the orphan with a mysterious past growing up to be the hero foretold by the ancient scrolls or whatever, which is really all Star Wars or Harry Potter are about. What makes a story great and memorable isn't built by its plot, or every jackhole with a Great Idea for a book would be a bestselling author. What makes a story worth telling and, more importantly, worth reading, is how it's told.

I never became a novelist, and my stabs at short fiction have been clumsy at best, but Lawrence Watt-Evans and Terry Pratchett opened me up to the idea of being a writer. They made it possible, and that was enough to kindle the flame. Then, a man came along who punched me in the gut, stole my milk money, and taught me everything I ever needed to know about anything.

I was in high school when it happened - I can't remember the year, exactly - and I was still a huge nerd. I read comic books and painted RPG miniatures in my spare time when I wasn't busy playing video games or reading nerdy literature, so I spent a lot of time in my local comic book store. Normally, it only stocked comics and RPG material - common stuff for any self-respecting comics shop - but, one day, a book appeared on the New Releases shelf. An actual book. Hardback, with a dust cover and everything. I didn't understand.

Curious as to why it was there more than anything else, I picked it up and gave it a quick glance. Harlan Ellison, it read at the top, a name before the title. Edgeworks. Volume 3: The Harlan Ellison Hornbook | Harlan Ellison's Movie.

Who the hell was Harlan Ellison, and why was his name on the same book three times on the cover alone? I had to know, so I took the book over to one of the more secluded corners of the shop and cracked it open.

That's when everything changed.

My fate was sealed.

The Harlan Ellison Hornbook turned out to be a collection of essays, which was something I didn't even know existed outside of the fabled five paragraph persuasive essays my freshman English teacher drilled into our heads every day of my ninth grade year. But these weren't normal essays. They were funny and sharp. Dangerous. Pointy. Brilliant.

I bought the book immediately and read it in one sitting. Nothing would ever be the same after that.

Lawrence Watt-Evans might have taught me the subtleties of storytelling, and Terry Pratchett showed me the wisdom in satire, but Harlan? Harlan took otherwise innocent words and weaponized them. I was enthralled.

I'd eventually move on to reading his equally dangerous fiction, but there was something about the essay format that grabbed me and just never let go.

From there, I moved on to other essayists/columnists: Mark Twain, H. L. Menken, P. J. O'Rourke, Hunter Thompson, Dave Barry, Erma Bombeck, Nora Ephron, and Dorothy Parker, just to name a few.

Reading Ellison also led me to more fiction writers, like Neil Gaiman, who somehow manages to effortlessly weave timeless stories into delicate narrative strands that bend and swim in the sunlight as you read them in a way that makes me feel inferior just by being in their presence. (*Sidenote*: When I found out Gaiman and Pratchett had collaborated on a little book called Good Omens, I nearly killed a man as I drove my crappy first car to the bookstore way too fast.)

However, despite my love of reading, at some point, I started putting more and more distance between myself and fiction. I still read Lawrence Watt-Evans, I still re-read Terry Pratchett, I still read Gaiman and Ellison and a little Douglas Adams when I'm in the mood, but I mostly stick to non-fiction these days. Essays.

When the internet came along, it opened me up to a whole new world of brilliant essayists, even though they'd started calling themselves bloggers by then. Jenny Lawson writes about the hilarious sadness (and furious happiness) of mental health over at thebloggess.com, Allie Brosh created the model of the modern memoir at Hyperbole and a Half, and Michele Poston Combs somehow finds poignant humor in things like parental narcissism and menopause at Rubber Shoes in Hell - and these are just a few of my favorites that spring to mind, although I have plenty more I've just picked up along the way at sites like Cracked and McSweeney's, or random Google searches. There are more essays being written now than ever before, and it's hard to keep up.

My love of reading eventually aligned with the rise of the internet and I started a blog of my own, which led to a career in journalism and becoming a columnist myself. I'll never work on the same level as anyone I've mentioned in this post, but I'm pretty happy with what I come up with, every now and then.

Even when nobody reads it.

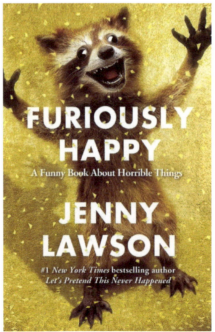

Chapter Twelve

Since I devoted the last chapter to the books that made me, you might think I'd be tempted to use this one to talk about the movies I grew up watching, and you'd be right. I *was* tempted, but only up until I realized that everyone already knows the movies. Seriously, pick a random nerd flick from the '80s and '90s and it's a reasonably safe bet it'd be on my list. Star Wars and Indiana Jones probably had the biggest impacts on me, but after that it's pretty standard cheesy '80s stuff. Ghostbusters, Karate Kid, Superman I and II. That sort of thing.

I guess the one movie most people have probably forgotten about that was a pretty big deal for me as a kid was Space Camp. I wanted to be an astronaut, so I more or less considered it a documentary of what I'd experience myself, if only my parents would let me go to the real Space Camp. They never did, but we did visit when passing through the area one time. It was like looking at everything I ever wanted and not being able to touch any of it.

So, nah. This chapter isn't going to be about movies. It's not going to be about anything, really. Because it's the last chapter.

I know! I'm sorry! But here's the thing. If I included every chapter I'd originally planned, the printing costs would keep most people from being able to buy this book. Seriously, being an indie author is tricky. Printing costs per page and every page in this book is oversized and in full color, which isn't cheap. (Nor was working on it easy. I've published three other books and none of them involved the level of layout issues and technical problems this one brought with it. Being an indie author is a lot like how I imagine it is to be an indie game developer, working on every part of the game yourself. Or, if I'm honest, I like to pretend it feels like being an early game developer, when one person could effectively code a game, then create all of its art assets, design its environments, write its lore, and everything else in between. So in a way, I kind of feel a kinship with some of my heroes when I independently publish.)

Maybe that's just me being weird again. I dunno. I never can tell.

Instead of movies or more games, this chapter is about wrapping everything up and telling you about what's coming next. I'm ending this book around 1993, the year I graduated high school. I seemed like a good stopping point not only because of how the whole graduation thing is a significant milestone in anyone's life, but because first person shooters and, more importantly, 3D accelerated graphics started becoming a serious thing shortly thereafter. And then a little thing called the internet came along…

I hope you've enjoyed this little trip down memory lane as much as I enjoyed writing it. The important points I want to leave you with are pretty simple. Gaming isn't just a hobby. I mean, it is, but it's much more than that. The interactive nature of gaming pulls you into other worlds like nothing else can. Sure, you can lose yourself in good book or a movie, but something about being able to move in and around and actually affect the worlds you explore in games has a special kind of power to it. And the really cool part is that the power never goes away, no matter how many years it's been since you last played your favorite games.

Stick around after this chapter ends to check out My Top 10 PC Games of All The Years bonus feature. It's not quite "all the years" *yet* since it only goes up to 1993, but the rest of the years are coming up in the next two books. When working on the list and deciding which games I wanted to include, I actually went back and replayed as many of them as possible, and you know what? Most of them not only held up, but took me right back to whatever age I was when I first played them. You know how certain smells can instantly conjure up a vivid memory you've long since forgotten about? It was kind of like that, only more real.

Playing Ultima II (spoilers: it's on the list) put me right back in the ugly orange swivel chair I used as a computer chair for most of my childhood. It was ripped a little on the front and the stuffing was poking out at odd angles, and I swear I could feel that one weird spring that used to stick me in all the wrong places whenever I wasn't careful sitting down. I could see my room in my parents' old house, probably not exactly how it really was back then, but exactly how I remember it being. If I focused on the screen, I could see my bookshelves from the corner of my eye, lined with Star Wars action figures and G.I. Joes. I could close my eyes and hear my mom talking on the old kitchen phone with the enormous coiled cord we had. I could smell her perfume.

She passed away in 2016.

Games were there for me when I was a kid and needed them, and they're still here for me as an adult whenever I need them again. I can be the Avatar of the Eight Virtues, righting wrongs and inspiring the people of Britannia whenever I want. I can load up Ultima VII and see all my old friends again: Iolo, Shamino, Dupree. I can hop in an X-Wing and save the galaxy from the evil Empire. I can beat Nazis to the Holy Grail and solve the mysteries of Atlantis. I can be a king on a quest, a cop on a quest, or a hero on a quest whenever the urge hits me.

Because games are time machines.

Sure, they can transport us to ancient eras or far-flung science fiction and fantasy realms in their own narratives, but they can also take us backward along the years of our own lifetimes in a kind of Quantum Leap way. They can take us back to a time when life was simpler, even when it was harder. They can bring back loved ones, if only for a quick glimpse. They can rekindle old passions and reignite the flames of imagination the world has spent years trying to extinguish as we grew up. They can take us back to a time of childlike wonder, when the simple act of seeing something you typed show up on a computer screen was amazing.

10 PRINT "KRISTIAN RULEZ!"

20 GOTO 10

Who didn't do that, back in the day? I remember the magic of The New Frontier and, in the end, our memories are all any of us have. They might fade with time, but games can bring them back, restore their vitality, and show us our past in living color. All we have to do is play them.

Why not go play some now?

Bonus Feature:
My Top 10 PC Games of All the Years

The full version of this list encompasses around thirty solid years of gaming, with my top ten PC games of each year for a total of somewhere around 300 titles. It's huge and writing it was daunting, but it's the most comprehensive history of gaming's high points as any I've seen.

Of course, this isn't the full version of the list because the whole thing would take up an entire book by itself. Since I'm dividing the Life Bytes series into three books, this part only goes as far as 1993, the year I graduated high school.

Yeah, I'm old.

It begins in the mid-80s, when I got my first computer for Christmas. It was an Apple][clone and I loved it, but I'm limiting the entirety of my Apple gaming to just ten games. The list really begins in 1988, when I got my first IBM-compatible PC and entered the Real Gamer demographic. I'm also trying to only include PC-exclusive games that weren't available on consoles, although that starts to get pretty tricky after 2005/2006 when the Xbox 360 and Playstation 3 were released.

It's also a list of *my* top ten games of each year, so it's not necessarily made up of the objectively best games. All that's here are the games I played and enjoyed at the time, that made an impression on me one way or another, for better or worse. Remakes, reboots, and remasters won't be included, either. Your favorite game will probably be omitted too, because it's *my* list and people like different things. You can just go make your own Top 10 if you feel that strongly about Speedball 2. Nobody's stopping you.

Now go! Gather your party and venture forth. Seventy games await you in The Early Years of this massive list. (You'll need to buy Life Bytes parts two and three for the whole thing. Sorry, but I gots ta eat too, you know.)

The Apple][Years
1982 - 1987

#10 – In Search of the Most Amazing Thing

I pretty much said everything that needs to be said about this game back in Chapter Two, but in case you're skipping around, here are the highlights. This was the first computer game I ever played on my own PC (and yes, Apples were still considered Personal Computers back then because the stupid "I'm a Mac and I'm a PC" ad campaign hadn't happened yet). It was a weird game and the ending was stupid, but it was fun for the time and will always have a special place in my memory.

None of it made any sense at all, though.

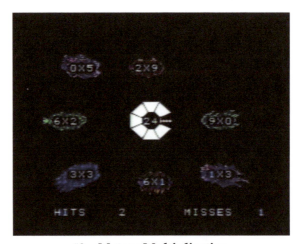

#9 – Meteor Multiplication

I don't have much to say about this one, other than the fact that my parents were big on the edutainment back in the day. This whole game consists of blasting meteors by way of multiplying the numbers on them, I guess because your space laser won't fire without doing math first. Seems like crappy space laser design to me, but whatever. It was kind of fun, I guess.

#8 – The Oregon Trail

"You have died of dysentery."

Do I even need to say anything about this one? The Oregon Trail has entered meme status these days, so everyone has either already played it or knows it well enough to not bother reading whatever I feel like saying about it.

I never did make it to Oregon, though.

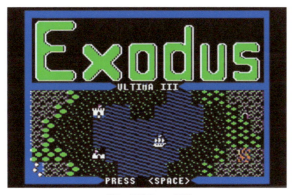

#7 – Ultima III

Ultima III was a kind of transitional fossil between Akalabeth and the first two Ultimas as the series was evolving into what it would become starting with Ultima IV. This one is probably my least favorite in the series (not counting Ultima 8 but not Ultima IX because, as I've said, the latter was actually a much better game at the time than people pretend it wasn't these days), although I'm not sure why. It was slightly less crazy than Ultima II but not nearly as grounded as Ultima IV. And you defeated the big bad guy with punch cards, which…yeah. I still don't really get it, either. My dad and I still played it together, but we wouldn't obsess over an Ultima again until, well, I'll get to that in a minute.

AND CONQUER TIME ITSELF TO BATTLE
MINAX THE ENCHANTRESS

#6 – Ultima II

Ultima II was not only the first Ultima I ever played, but it was also the first real RPG I ever experienced. It was a game with an identity crisis, not knowing if it was swords and sorcery or spaceships and pew-pew lasers, but something about it just clicked with me. Maybe it was the cloth map and the manuals that drew me into the world. Maybe it was the moongates that hopped you around through time on a recreation of Earth throughout history and the distant future. Maybe it was how we lived in Texas and San Antonio somehow made it into the game. I'm not sure, but my dad and I loved it.

I already covered this in Chapter Three, but to recap, Ultima II was the game that brought me and my Dad closer together for the first time since playing that stupid football game on the Channel F. We played it co-op before co-op existed, discussing the world and the clues we picked up and wrote down in our notebooks, dissecting the mysteries of the time gates (I can't actually remember if they were called time gates of moongates in Ultima II, but they'd become moongates eventually, so I guess let's stick with that), and generally enjoying the heck out of it together.

It started a lifetime of this sort of thing, me and my dad bonding together as gamers. Skipping ahead for a minute, we played everything together over the years. Eventually, we each had a computer and set up a home network so we could shoot each other in Doom and have our armies face off in Warcraft. One memorable game of Age of Empires sticks in my mind as we were pretty evenly matched as far as our skill levels, so the whole thing was kind of a perpetual draw that came down to both of us having exactly one peasant left with no resources on the map. The entire game came down to whoever could find the one remaining tree on the planet to train up the cheapest military unit possible.

It lasted hours.

Thanks to gaming together, my dad and I managed to skip most of the father-son drama other people tend to get up to whenever the kid turns into an angst-ridden teenager no one understands, and it all goes back to Ultima II.

I'll never forget that.

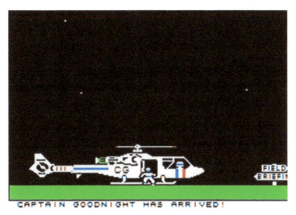

#5 – Captain Goodnight and the Islands of Fear

Captain Goodnight had some of the best animation in any game up to that point, although I was never quite sure of what I was supposed to be doing while playing it. I just enjoyed watching the little guy run across the screen because I was young, computers were still new, and I was easily amused. I never made it very far, but I do remember that Captain Midnight was always "undaunted" by my clumsy efforts because the game made sure to tell me every time he came back to life and returned to the fray.

Poor Captain Midnight. He deserved better than me.

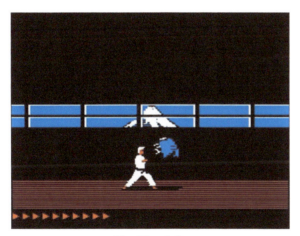

#4 – Karateka

Did I just say Captain Midnight had some of the best animation in any game? What I meant was it had really good animation, but the best in the business (at the time) went to Karateka, hands down. For a boy briefly obsessed with The Karate Kid, this game was absolute perfection. Just run to the right and fight whatever gets in your way with the power of Karate. Even if the only thing in your way was a stupid murder bird you could barely ever defeat.

Did anyone else insist on bowing before every encounter, or was it just me?

Just me, then. Okay. Good to know.

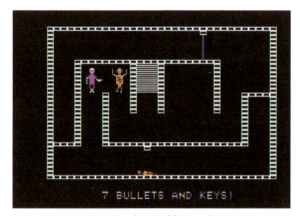

#3 – Castle Wolfensetin

Predating Wolfenstein 3D by a little over a decade, the original Castle Wolfenstein was probably the first stealth game ever made. The goal, as it is in Wolfenstein 3D, was to escape the titular castle, the difference being that this one involved more sneaking than shooting. It also featured some of the first speech in any game, which was an impressive technological accomplishment considering the squeaks and squawks that normally came out of my computer's tinny little squawkbox.

While the regular soldiers were easy enough to deal with when you had to, the SS were absolute beasts. They were protected by bulletproof vests and resistant to your threats, plus they'd chase you from room to room once you were detected. The regular guards didn't do that, I guess because they were overworked and underpaid and just didn't feel like chasing an escaping prisoner was worth all the extra effort if they weren't getting overtime.

The game also involved a lot of looting various chests left scattered about by Nazi scum, which were often inexplicably filled with bratwurst for some weird reason I never understood but that was probably just some kind of German kink my inexperienced American mind couldn't understand.

I don't think I ever actually made it out of the castle, though. There was also a lot of waiting, which was kind of weird for the time. Searching a dead guard took time, but opening chests could take ages and you never knew whether you were going to get something useful like an enemy uniform or something worthless, like a bunch of cannonballs. You could always try to save time by shooting the lock on the chest, but you ran the risk of it being filled with explosives and, well, exploding. The gunshot could also attract nearby SS Stormtroopers, so it was never really a valid option.

But I was an impatient kid, so…I died a lot. Often from exploding chests.

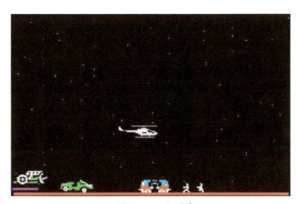

#2 – Rescue Raiders

My dad absolutely adored this game. He played it incessantly, any chance he could. To this day, I swear he would eat his dinner faster than me just so he could truck it into my room and take over the computer before I could finish not eating my vegetables.

In fact, Rescue Raiders might be one of the main reasons I got good grades in school, because I always had time to do my homework. My dad made sure of it. And, just to make sure I was motivated, he'd sit and play this game the entire time I was diagramming sentences or learning what kind of mud was historically used to create bricks or something because a lot of what kids learn in school is useless nonsense.

As soon as I finished my homework, I could have a turn on the computer – but if I took too long, it'd be time for my shower and then bed, so I better hurry up. After all, look how much fun my dad was having getting in all the computer time he wanted.

The game itself was actually really good and I wasn't awful at it, for once. It was almost a real time strategy game before there were real time strategy games in the sense that you could decide the build order of different vehicles that would move from one side of the screen to the other. Some would help you fight the enemy helicopter while others were good for stopping the bad guy's vehicles he was deploying from his side of the screen that were headed toward yours.

You helicopter was armed bullets and bombs, the latter of which would come streaming out the bottom of your flying machine in a very satisfying line of digital death.

The game also taught me that Cherbourg was a real place that existed, since it was always the first battleground during any game. I probably never made it past it, though. I didn't entirely suck at the game, but that doesn't mean I was actually good at it or anything, though.

But my dad was.

#1 – Ultima IV

Ultima IV was the game that changed everything. While I'd enjoyed questing around Earth in Ultima II and Sosaria in Ultima III, it wasn't until the fourth game in the series that everything really clicked into place. The series really seemed to find itself in Ultima IV, whereas it was more of a mishmash of different ideas in the previous games. Ultima IV introduced Britannia and established a real sense of identity and place for the first time.

After Ultima IV, playing every new entry in the series felt like coming home. I had friends who lived there, people I cared about and who cared about me. In my mind, anyway. I was a weird kid. I didn't fit in with any group and was always on the outside, alone with my thoughts and lost in my own imagination. Ultima helped me at a time when I really needed to feel like I belonged somewhere, which probably sounds way less pathetic than it actually was, but the series gave me that.

Not only did I get to play it with my dad, but I found friends in its little digital people and managed to rekindle the childlike sense of magic and wonder that was already being snuffed out by the time Ultima IV came around when I was ten years old. The world has a way of doing that to people, but this goofy little game series helped me hold on to mine, and I'll always be grateful for that.

When not playing the game, usually whenever my mom would insist that I go outside and get some exercise like a normal kid, I'd be out in my backyard pretending I was exploring Britannia with my fellowship of companions. I'd mix reagents (usually whatever dirt, grass, weeds, and rocks I could find) and cast spells an imagined foes. I knew it wasn't real, so don't look at me like that. I just enjoyed pretending.

And I still do. Maybe that's a bad thing, I dunno. I've never been very good at being an adult, so I wouldn't be able to tell, either way. All I know is that I sometimes make things up for a living and I don't think I'd be able to do that if Ultima IV hadn't shown me that having an active imagination could make the world a better place. Whether it was learning valuable life lessons by aspiring toward the eight virtues like the Avatar I played in the game, or just finding the value in playing make believe, Ultima IV had whatever secret sauce I needed to help get me through some pretty rough years.

With my dad right beside me the whole time.

Thanks, Ultima.

The Early PC Years (1998-1993)

<u>1988</u>

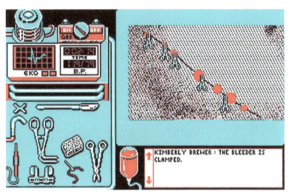

#10 - Life & Death

I beat Doogie Howser to surgeonhood by a full year by playing this game. Neil Patrick Harris wouldn't start suturing patients until 1989, and his character was 16 when the show started. I was only 13 the first time I started up Life & Death and immediately murdered a patient. I forgot to administer any anesthetic before I cut into him, so he screamed out in agony and promptly died.

I never did get the hang of this game because screw it, I was only 13 years old. I still had a lot of fun trying, though. And the lamentations of my patients never got old.

#9 - Rocket Ranger

This game. My first PC was an 8088 with an EGA monitor, which I thought made me pretty hot stuff, until I bought Rocket Ranger based on the screenshots on the back of its box. After I got back home and installed it, I realized EGA was actually pretty crap. The screenshots were from the Amiga version, and they were beautiful. However, the image on my monitor was limited to 16 colors of sadness.

The game was still great fun, though. Flying around, zapping Nazis, falling on your face over and over when you can't manage to take off because you suck at life. Running out of fuel and crashing on your way to save the day because you didn't read the code wheel right. Good times.

#8 - Battle Chess

I've always enjoyed chess, but I've never been very good at it. I do like to laugh at people who think that mastering the game is some sign of superior intelligence rather than just being really good at a game though, and nothing was funnier than playing Battle Chess. All of the little animations were genuinely comical to my 13-year-old brain, and I'm sure I remember more than one crotch-shot, which was pretty much the pinnacle of human achievement in comedy as far as I was concerned.

The only problem with Battle Chess was that after you'd seen every animation for the hundred billionth time, they just got annoying. I'd eventually switch them off, but then I'd realize that I was just playing chess at that point, which was pretty darn boring. There isn't a lot of staying power in this classic, but the fun times are pretty great. Until they're not.

#7 - Battlehawks 1942

The first in Lucasfilm's WWII flight sim series, Battlehawks 1942 was as fun to play as it was to not. That's because it came with a big, spiral-bound manual filled with all sorts of WWII facts and tidbits. One of the best ways to play the game was to read through a bit of the manual to get psyched up, then hop into the game to shoot down some baddies. I played it a lot with my dad, who was always better at it than I was. The jerk.

This game also ignited my interest in WWII history, which would continue through college when I accidentally signed up for a graduate level course as a freshman. I managed to pass, but just barely. Ah, memories.

#6 - BattleTech: The Crescent Hawk's Inception

Outside of Ultima II (which I played on my Apple][clone), I never knew you could combine sci-fi and RPGs until I played this game. The title screen was much cooler than anything the actual game had to offer, but it was still a lot of fun. I never made it very far because it was kind of complicated, I was only 13, and I didn't have a manual for it because reasons. Still, I always had fun trying to figure out what the heck I was doing in a universe I didn't understand.

Plus, giant robots.

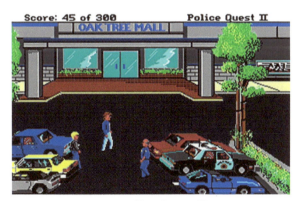
#5 - Police Quest II

They don't make games like Police Quest today. And they didn't really make them like Police Quest back when they made Police Quest. Sierra went out on a limb with this series, and it usually paid off. I wouldn't play the first game until years after I played part two, but it's just as well. The first one was super short and focused on the mundane routine of an officer's life (which was way more fun than it sounds). The sequel improved on that, and by the time Police Quest III came out, I was pretty sure the series was going to be around forever. Then Daryl Gates happened, and it wasn't anymore.

#4 - Wasteland

I never really got into the whole post-apocalyptic genre until Fallout 3 came along in 2008 which is probably heresy or something, but I don't really care. I played the original Fallout games and, while I enjoyed them, they really weren't as good as people remember. Or at least as I remember them. But Wasteland was Fallout before Fallout was Fallout and it was a much better game. Maybe it's because the limited EGA color palette kept the game from seeming too brown and broken-down and, well, post-apocalyptic, but Wasteland played and felt more or less like any other RPG at the time, just with knives instead of swords and guns in place of bows.

The most interesting part was actually how it worked in both copy protection and saved on the premium of floppy disc space. At certain points in the game, you had to bust out the manual to read various paragraphs describing what was going on. I don't know what it was about needing to look things up in a book that went so well with early games, but it probably had something to do with blending analog and digital together. Maybe it was a transitional thing that eased us into the all-digital world we live in now, or maybe it was just plain better. Either way, it helped bring the game world alive in a way that the graphics couldn't at the time, and I thought that was pretty neat.

#3 - Manhunter: New York

Manhunter was one of the weirdest games Sierra ever made. It's set in a dystopian, post-apocalyptic version of New York after giant intergalactic eyeballs have enslaved humanity and forced everyone to dress as monks or something. It was never very clear. It was also the first point and click adventure game I'd ever played, since it did away with Sierra's traditional text parser in favor of a 1st person slideshow view more like we'd see in Myst years later. I spent hours trying to figure this game out, but mostly I just wandered around and died a lot. My most distinct memory comes from very early on (which is about as far as I ever got), where I was able to do the knife/hand thing I saw Bishop do in Aliens. So that was cool.

#2 - Ultima V: Warriors of Destiny

I've played and completed every Ultima game...except Ultima V. It was actually one of the first games I bought after getting my first PC, since I'd been unable to run it on my Apple][clone due to the game wanting a crazy amount (64k) of RAM. I only had 48k, so it'd play the intro but always crash afterward. Which sucked, because Ultima V is widely regarded as being one of the best entries in the series.

So why didn't I ever complete it? Or even get very far? A couple of reasons, really. The biggest one probably has to do with my top game of 1988. Once I found it, I had very little time for anything else. But the second reason is that Ultima VI was just around the corner...

#1 - Maniac Mansion

This game changed everything for me. Heck, it changed everything for everyone. Multiple characters, multiple endings, a point-and-click interface. Humor. Maniac Mansion had it all.

Once I discovered it, I never went back. All the Sierra games were suddenly clunky nightmares of keyboard controls and fiddly text parsers, and I wanted nothing more to do with them. I also didn't want more serious narratives or overly fanciful, saccharine fairy tale nonsense. I wanted good jokes, funny characters, and skewed humor.

I wanted...Lucasfilm Games.

<u>1989</u>

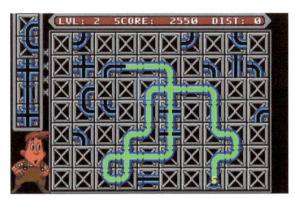

#10 - Pipe Dream

Lucasfilm Games didn't just stick to one or two genres, back in its early days. It tried its hand at a number of different games, sometimes developing them in-house, and sometimes buying up an existing property to publish. Pipe Dream was originally released for the Amiga under the name Pipe Mania. Lucasfilm grabbed it, ported it to other platforms, and called it Pipe Dream.

It was a fun time killer that could get pretty challenging for my budding young intellect. You might remember having played it every single time you hacked a machine in Bioshock.

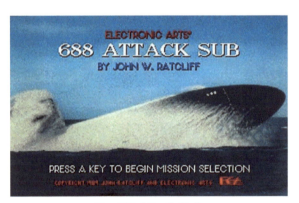

#9 - 688 Attack Sub

I sucked at this game, but boy was it fun. I never had any idea what I was doing, since I was again playing a game sans manual. (Hey, I was 14. BBSs were a thing, and I was friends with a lot of sysops. Sysops who had "special" file sections for trusted users. Don't judge me.)

It was far too complicated for my stupid newly-teenaged brain to quite grasp. There were lots of controls and fiddly systems, and I just wanted to blow things up. But something about figuring out how to make the game do anything was part of the fun, which I guess was the case with a lot of old games.

#8 - Populous

My first god sim. Everyone's first god sim. There's not much to say about Populous that hasn't already been said before. I liked it for the same reasons everyone else liked it. You got to play as a god, you had little worshipers you could smite at will, and you could murder everyone. Or help them. Whichever.

I never did get the hang of raising and lowering land, though. And I never understood why a god would need to bother with such mundane levels of civic planning. Why not just set a bush on fire and command it to tell of one of your subjects to "Go ye forth and grab yonder shovel"?

Ah, well. It's still a fun game.

#7 - Hero's Quest / Quest for Glory 1

Hey, you got your RPG in my adventure game! No, you got your adventure game in my RPG!

Two genres that should have never worked together somehow blended like chocolate and peanut butter. Yeah, it still had Sierra's crappy interface and you died stupidly every five minutes, and you could get yourself into no-win scenarios like other people get into their clothes, but man was it a fun game. It was originally called Hero's Quest, but Sierra forgot to trademark the name. After Milton Bradley trademarked an electronic version of HeroQuest, they were forced to change the name to the now familiar Quest for Glory.

Sierra had a real thing for sticking Quest somewhere in their titles.

#6 - The Colonel's Bequest

The first in the long Laura Bow series of two whole games, this one was an absolute mess. It had a lot of timed events where you had to either follow characters or be in a certain spot at a specific time, and the puzzles were traditionally Sierra Stupid™. Yet, even with everything the game got wrong, it was still intriguing as hell.

It was a murder mystery, which we still don't have a lot of in today's gaming. It focused on characters rather than puzzles, and had an interesting story, even if it was mired in the typical bad puns and clichés of Sierra's writing.

#5 - Tunnels of Armageddon

Yet another game acquired from the dubious files section of a local BBS, this game had absolutely no point. I'm sure there was a story involved in some way, but whatever it was didn't matter. All you did was fly through these colorful tunnels while trying not to crash into walls and explode.

That was pretty much it. And it was awesome.

I used to put on some '80s heavy metal and then pretend I was an ace tunnel pilot in some alternate reality where tunnel pilots were a thing, and then I'd tear into the game for hours. If you manage to track this game down to give it a whirl - and I highly recommend it - be advised that a joystick is a must.

All the cool tunnel pilots have them. Don't you want to be cool, too?

#4 - SimCity

The original city planning game. What more is there to say? It birthed a genre, eventually led to The Sims, and you could build nightmare roadways to cause epic traffic jams. It was great.

I played a lot of this one, but mostly just when I was bored with all my other games and couldn't think of anything better to do. It would take a few sequels for the design to really come together, but there's still a quirky charm with how simple yet rewarding the first game can be.

#3 - Their Finest Hour: The Battle of Britain

I spent more hours with this flight sim than with any other action game I had on my PC, including Tunnels of Armageddon. It took everything that was great about Battlehawks 1942 and cranked it up to eleven. Or really, just 10. The eleven wouldn't come until the next game in the series, but Their Finest Hour was responsible for some of the best gaming memories with my dad that I have.

We played the Ultima games together, and we played Their Finest Hour. It was our thing.

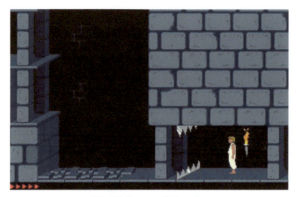

#2 - Prince of Persia

I desperately wanted a VGA card and monitor along with a sound card around the time I discovered the original Prince of Persia. I remember that distinctly, because a couple of the selling points of the game were that its EGA graphics weren't bad and it had surprisingly good PC speaker support, both of which just made me want VGA graphics and a sound card even more.

I never managed to save the princess or whatever because the game was crazy with its time limit and lack of saves, but everything else was awesome. The animation remains impressive to this day, and the sudden deaths from the various traps still make me laugh.

My favorite is the blade chomper of death. So good.

#1 - Indiana Jones and the Last Crusade Graphic Adventure

This was - and remains - THE BEST MOVIE TIE-IN GAME EVER MADE.

Yes, the caps were necessary. The Last Crusade is one of the most influential, yet overlooked point-and-click games ever, and I honestly don't understand why. It took the story from the movie, added a bunch of stuff (and cut out a little bit), then combined it all together into a great adventure game that didn't take itself too seriously.

It even came with an awesome copy of Henry Jones' Grail Diary, complete with little scribbled notes and coffee stains on the pages. It introduced dialog trees, and also eliminated no-win scenarios, and even in the one spot where you could die (while navigating the traps at the end of the game), it made a great joke out of it and you didn't lose any progress. You just tried again until you got it.

The design philosophy behind The Last Crusade would go on to dominate all subsequent Lucasfilm (later LucasArts) graphic adventures, along with the point-and-click genre as a whole. Eventually, even Sierra would get in on the game, even if they never managed to get it quite right.

Find this game. Play it. YOU ARE WELCOME.

1990

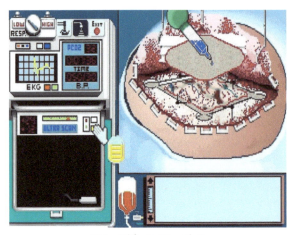

#10 - Life & Death 2

The year I finally got a VGA card, Life & Death 2 showed up with 256 color graphics and brain surgery. This one is even better than the last, because you can kinda sorta actually tell what you're doing once you've cut some poor soul's head open, which is nice.

These days, I can only think of it as a Ben Carson simulator, though. I played it a little bit last night, and every time I cut into someone, I shouted something about pyramid grain silos and then tried to cut the gay out of my patient's brain. Good times.

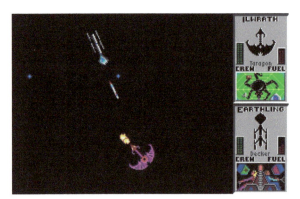

#9 - Star Control

This was a cool little game that had to wait until its sequel to really get good, but it was still fun. It's totally not a Star Trek simulator, though. And you totally don't use the Enterprise to shoot at Klingons or anything. Those are Ilwraths. Obviously.

It was mostly an arcade affair, though I remember there being a bit of light strategy involved, as well. Mostly, you set things up and then went into the pew-pew battle screen where you shot at other ships until they exploded. And that was pretty much it. And yet, it still somehow managed to become a huge time sink for me.

Go figure.

#8 - Worlds of Ultima: The Savage Empire

Origin tried to mix things up a little with the Ultima franchise by taking everything everyone had grown to love about the series and throwing it away. But it worked.

In the Worlds of Ultima games, of which there were only two, you still play as the Avatar, but aren't on Britannia. In Savage Empire, you're whisked away to the Valley of Eodon, which is basically the set piece of any given pulp fiction rag of yesteryear featuring a lost jungle world filled with giant insects and dinosaurs.

It wasn't a proper Ultima, but it was close enough to kill some time while I waited for Ultima VII to come out.

#7 - Quest for Glory 2

The second entry in the Quest for Glory series took the player away from the familiar tropes of European medieval fantasy and plopped you down in more of an Arabian Nights setting. It was a breath of fresh air at the time, and it all seemed super exotic.

If I went and replayed it today though, I'm pretty sure I'd notice all the stereotypes and subtle racism that was sort of an undercurrent in most Sierra titles that I was incapable of perceiving as a kid. Maybe not, but I don't want to replay it and take any chances.

Better safe than sorry.

#6 - It Came from the Desert

Another Cinemaware game, but this time I finally had a VGA monitor! After seeing this beauty running on a demo loop in my local software store for ages, I couldn't wait to buy it and run home to check out the amazing graphics I missed out on with Rocket Ranger.

I installed the game, ran the executable, and then...EGA graphics. Again.

The store had been running the Amiga version, of course, and Cinemaware hadn't bothered to start adding 256-color graphics to their PC ports yet, so I was screwed again. I still enjoyed the game and put a lot of hours into it, but I learned to never trust screenshots again.

#5 - King's Quest V

I hadn't played a King's Quest game in ages when this one came out, but I was suckered in by Sierra's new engine. VGA graphics! Point and click interface! All the cool things!

It's too bad its puzzles were awful, but the worst part about the game was how they hadn't fully embraced point and click yet. No, you didn't move around with the keyboard anymore, and yes, you clicked where you wanted to go and your little dude went there, but...he didn't always. Because Sierra loved killing the player ALL THE DANG TIME, you had to click in just the right spot and make a million little clicks so King Graham could walk inch-by-inch through a screen because you couldn't rely on his pathfinding to not have him plummet to his death from off a cliff.

Fortunately, the original version of this game came on floppies because CD-ROMs weren't a thing yet, which meant I only had to read the bad dialog rather than hear it "acted" out by whoever happened to be walking by Roberta Williams' office on their way to the bathroom that day.

#4 - Ultima VI: The False Prophet

I have a deep and unyielding love for the Ultima series, so you might be wondering why Ultima VI isn't higher up on the list of my top games from 1990. It's pretty simple, really. It just didn't grab me like the other entries in the series. There wasn't anything wrong with the game - and, in many ways, it was much better than all of the previous games.

But for whatever reason, it just didn't grab hold of me like, say, Ultima IV did or Ultima VII would a couple of years later. I think it mostly had to do with the user interface. It was pretty clunky, but it was also the first mouse-driven Ultima game, so I cut it some slack. It did some things better and some things worse, but the story was still great. And all my old friends were back, so I didn't mind too much.

#3 - Loom

My big Christmas present in 1990 was a sound card, along with two Lucasfilm Games. Loom was one of them, and it was the perfect showcase for my new Sound Blaster card since the entire game is based around using music to cast magic spells.

The game was short and obviously planned to be the first in a new series that never materialized, but it was magical. It was designed by Brian Moriarty, who also designed Wishbringer, one of my favorite

Infocom titles. The game even came with an audio cassette containing a radio drama setting up the game world and your place in it.

I lost count of how many times I listened to that thing.

#2 - Wing Commander

A friend of mine gave me a copy of this game, and I was immediately hooked. So was my dad. We used to fight over who got computer time, just to play it. It had everything: a great soundtrack, awesome graphics, a cool branching storyline. It was a Star Wars sim before there was a Star Wars sim, and I loved it.

Unfortunately, since I had a new VGA monitor, I used to enjoy playing my games in EGA mode for a few minutes, just to appreciate how much better the graphics were on my new rig. For most games, this was fine. I'd check out EGA, laugh at all the dithered red people, then pop back over to VGA and relish my graphical snobbery. However, the way Wing Commander changed graphics modes was by way of overwriting the VGA files with EGA ones, which meant that once I'd converted it to EGA, it was stuck that way until I was able to get another copy from my friend.

When my dad came home later that day and tried to play a game, he was...displeased.

#1 - The Secret of Monkey Island

Another year, another Lucasfilm game in the top spot. But no one can argue with this choice. The Secret of Monkey Island was an even better showcase for my new Sound Blaster card than Loom, with a much better soundtrack that I still listen to and love to this very day. (The main theme is even my wife's ringtone on my phone.)

Everything about the game was great. EVERYTHING.

The puzzles were fun. The dialog was sharp. The characters were fully realized. The music was amazing. The graphics were crisp.

I was in love.

1991

#10 - Lemmings

Ah, Lemmings. Many countless hours were devoted to both saving and annihilating these little fools, in equal measure. There's a reason this game has seen so many iterations and sequels over the years: it's dang addictive. Even today, starting up the original game risks me losing oceans of time to it. I can't play just one level, and I always have to just see what the next level looks like after I beat one.

Until I get super frustrated and just nuke them all, that is.

Which kind of happens a lot, actually.

#9 - Night Shift

I still love this game, and I still play it fairly regularly.

Another one of Lucasfilm Games' dips into the wading pool of other genres, Night Shift was developed by a third party who brought it to Lucasfilm. They rebranded it and published it as a toy factory making Star Wars and Lucasfilm Games related action figures.

You play as a guy or a girl charged with keeping The Machine working, which is a crazy, multi-storied contraption that's constantly failing in spectacular ways.

The toy company is called Industrial Might and Logic instead of Industrial Light and Magic, and the title screen of the game is a clever modification of ILM's old wizard logo. There are also lemmings involved, but not the suicidal kind from other games or any of Disney's fake True Life Adventure movies.

There are two of the little beasts in this game: one that slows you down by humping your leg, and another who runs around and mucks up the machine. Then, there's an angry lawyer who constantly tries to bludgeon you with the hammer of litigation or whatever, so it's a constant race up and down the machine, repairing what's broken and trying to keep everything in sync.

It starts out pretty simple but gets really crazy before you get to the end of the game, which explains why I've never made it to the end of the game. I've been trying for a couple of decades now, but I only ever manage to progress one or two levels every few years. Maybe by the time I die, I'll have completed it.

But probably not.

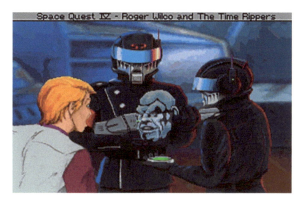

#8 - Space Quest IV

This was the first Space Quest game I played, because it had VGA graphics and a point and click interface. For whatever reason, the series just didn't appeal to me any sooner. I remember looking at the screenshots of SQIV before I had my VGA monitor and was longing for one with my nose pressed up against the pages of a Computer Shopper magazine like a Dickensian street urchin peering at day-old bread in a bakery window, imagining that I could never get bored with a game that looked that good.

Unfortunately, it was still a Sierra game. It was funnier than other Sierra games, and even the multiple deaths were kind of endearing, but it was still filled with the same no-win states and lousy design decisions that plagued almost every Sierra title. The last straw for me was probably around the time I found their little joke about Loom, which was one of my favorite games. It was basically Sierra taking a stab at Lucasfilm's design philosophy, and it irked me. I never did complete the game, but it wasn't for lack of trying.

I just eventually gave up. You know, like with life.

#7 - Eye of the Beholder

This was the game that taught me I have absolutely no sense of direction. It was super cool and super Dungeons & Dragons, which was a pen-and-paper RPG I always wanted to play, but never got a chance to on account of not really having many friends because I'm a giant weirdo.

Booting up Eye of the Beholder for the first time was a revelation, because I could finally play D&D instead of just sitting in my closet alone, reading sourcebooks and pretending I had friends.

Unfortunately, the stepped slideshow movement and making my own graph paper maps proved far too daunting a task, and I just ended up getting lost and dying a lot.

It didn't stop me from playing, though. Or from playing the next game in the series. Or the next one.

While getting lost and dying in each and every one of them.

I suck.

#6 - The Adventures of Willy Beamish

The tagline for this game was something along the lines of, "Who wouldn't want to be 9 years old again?", which was weird because I'd just been nine years old, like, 7 years earlier. But whatever, I was already nostalgic. Plus, this game looked like a freaking cartoon, which was amazing back in 1991. I bought it immediately.

It wasn't as open as other adventure games, because you couldn't just click to walk anywhere. You could only click on interactive objects and room exit points, but it was still a great technological achievement.

The story is about an evil corporation pumping sludge into the town's water supply or something, and it's up to Willy Beamish, his gang of treehouse pals, and his pet frog, Horny, to save the day. And somehow win the Totally Not Nintendo (Nintari) world championship along the way.

I haven't played it in years, so I honestly have no idea how well it holds up today, but I loved it way back when. I think it was even ported to the Nintendo DS not too long ago. I should probably try to track a down a copy.

#5 - Police Quest III

The creeping racism of Sierra really started to bubble up to the surface with some of the traffic stops in this game, but solving the main storyline was a lot of fun. It's basically the same as the other Police Quest games, but with VGA graphics along with point-and-click gameplay.

I don't remember any no-win situations exactly, but I do know you could screw up some of your traffic stops when they went to court if you didn't exactly follow proper police procedure. Which is weird, because this was California in the '90s, when proper police procedure was basically just, "Beat up all the black guys and then lie about it later."

Which is kinda still the procedure, really.

The next game in the series was called Open Season, which was "designed" by Daryl Gates and filled with racism and horrible full motion video. Seriously, the game was awful. Just awful.

But PQ3 was still fun. I replayed it not too long ago and still enjoyed it, even if I winced at a few characterizations.

Here's a friendly tip to everyone on the planet: Don't try to write in dialect. Ever. Unless you're Mark Twain or an actual person of color, just don't do it. Your work will come across as insensitive at best, and downright racist at worst.

And it's usually the worst.

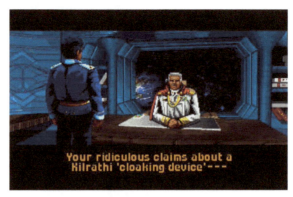

#4 - Wing Commander II

Same as Wing Commander I, only better.

What else is there to say? It was the last great hurrah before Chris Roberts' Hollywood envy would drive him down the dark, dark road of FMV. And then actually to Hollywood, where he made the Wing Commander movie that we do not speak of. Ever. Seriously, there's nothing more to say here.

Besides, I KNOW THE DESTRUCTION OF THE TIGER'S CLAW WAS YOUR FAULT!

#3 - Secret Weapons of the Luftwaffe

The third and final game in Lucasfilm's WWII flight simulators was also its best. It took everything great about Battlehawks 1942 and Their Finest Hour, and cranked it up to eleven. (See? I told you it would.)

Better graphics, better sound, and experimental jets. The game had everything, and SWOTL was one of the last games my dad and I actively played together on a regular basis. I don't mean we played competitively or anything. He'd play his missions and I'd play mine, but we'd talk about them later and it was basically like playing the game together.

It was pretty much the 1991 version of co-op.

#2 - Civilization

I don't really need to write anything about this one, do I? We all know Civilization. Everyone knows Civilization. We all live it every day.

But Sid Meier squeezed it into a few floppies and unleashed the first real taste of gaming crack to the world. You don't just play a quick game of Civilization. You play epic games of Civilization that take as long as they need to in order for you to either vanquish your enemies or die trying.

Or maybe go for one of those namby-pamby non-military victories all the hippies seem to love so much.

Stupid hippies.

#1 - Monkey Island 2: LeChuck's Revenge

Monkey Island 2 remains the gold standard for adventure game design. Non-linear progression, interconnected puzzles, brilliant writing, great characters, multiple interesting locations, constant new art rewards, etc...

This game had it all.

I still love it so much, I used it to propose to my wife.

True story.

1992

#10 - Stunt Island

This is probably one of the least known titles on my entire list. Released by Disney, it was an odd combination of flight sim, movie maker, and non-linear video editing simulator. Whichever area was its focus depends on who you talk to.

Some people think it was first and foremost a flight simulator; specifically, a stunt flying simulator. You played the role of a pilot working for a movie studio, and it was your job to pull off various stunts and get the shot for a film. Other people think it's a movie creator, and all that stunt flying business is just one of the filmmaking tools the game gives you.

Whichever camp you fell into, it was a really fun game. Unique in every way, its flight model was a little wonky and its editing tools a bit clunky, but playing it taught you a little bit about a lot. You had to learn light scripting to move "actors" around in the world at the right times, light flight-simming to get your plane to do what you needed it to do without exploding, and light video editing to put it all together.

Stunt Island also used a fully polygonal 3D engine with Gouraud shading and was almost entirely coded in assembly, so chew on that. It also produced what was I think were probably the first recorded machinimas in gaming. But I can't prove that, so please don't write me angry letters about your awesome Halo videos or whatever.

I do know I was never very good at playing the game or making movies with it, so I'm probably not the best judge, either way.

#9 - Conquests of the Longbow: The Legend of Robin Hood

This Sierra game doesn't really feel like a Sierra game. It kind of plays like one, but it's actually really good. It's also one of their lesser-known titles, which is just inexplicable to me.

You play as Robin Hood, and you pretty much know the story from there. The game has the usual inventory-based puzzles of a traditional adventure game, but it also has little minigames like light archery and a medieval board game called Nine Men's Morris, which I became so obsessed with, I made my own board out of a piece of plywood and the wood-burning kit I had because I was a weird kid.

The game also opens with a lyrical intro, although the lyrics weren't sung by anyone because CD-ROMs weren't a thing yet, and Sierra would've probably just had Diana down in Purchasing sing it anyway because she was always going on about how great her church choir was or something.

Still, it was an original lyrical song opening a video game, which is the first time that ever happened, I think. Sierra would do it again the following year, but more on that when I get to '93.

#8 - Alone in the Dark

Lovecraftian horror meets the impossible geometry of 1992 polygonal characters. The true horror of this game obviously came from the LSD-infused visuals of Triangle Man beating Particle Cthulhu or whatever, but the rest of the game's scares weren't too shabby, either.

Beating Resident Evil to market by four years or so, Alone in the Dark was the very first survival horror game. It was slow and clunky and kind of goofy, but horror games without Elvira's cleavage in them were few and far between back in those days, so we took what we could get.

The sequels would get progressively ridiculous and awful as the years went on, so if you've ever had any curiosity about the series, play the first one first. It makes swallowing the spooky cowboy-shaped triangle people that come later go down a lot easier.

Yee-haw, ghost riders.

#7 - Quest for Glory III: Wages of War

More Quest for Glory!

Again, it's basically more of the same, but this time we leave the Arabian Nights setting and move on to Africa. Except it's called Fricana and is entirely populated by lion people. Which made sense, because there was a brief period in the early '90s when an African setting was all the rage, back before new age "spiritualism" crept in and made the appropriation of Native American traditions by white people a thing.

The '90s were a really weird time, y'all.

One of the lion people's names was Simba, who was even the son of the king if I remember correctly, but don't get your hopes up. Nobody ever holds him up on a rock to a rising crescendo of Elton John songs or anything.

The whole plot revolves around stopping a war between the lion people and the leopard people that's being orchestrated by an evil wizard who somehow isn't named Jaffar. Do that, and you save the day and are ready to move on to the next Quest for Glory, which I never actually played. I keep meaning to though, so that's got to count for something, right?

Right?

#6 - Wizardry VII: Crusaders of the Dark Savant

I'm almost ashamed to admit it, but this was my first Wizardry game. It had some really great music, and creating my characters at the start was detailed and a lot of fun. Then, the story happened and I had no idea what was going on.

There was something about spaceships and intergalactic overlords, and then there was crashing on a medieval planet or something, and none of it made any sense, but I'm pretty sure it was about Scientology.

Fun game. Played it a lot. Got lost and died, mostly. Basically, it was Eye of the Beholder all over again, but with the occasional space alien rat monster.

#5 - Star Trek: 25th Anniversary

Who knew that Star Trek would lend itself so well to the adventure game format? Star Trek: 25th Anniversary and its sequel, Judgment Rites, proved that the franchise could not only work as an adventure game, but was incredibly well suited for it.

As long as you pretended the atrocious, real-time starships-as-nimble-fighters battle segments didn't happen, anyway. Because they were awful. (They're even more awful if you try to play them through DOSBox today because you'll never get the CPU timing quite right and they'll either crawl along at a slideshow's pace or whiz by so fast you'll never have time to fire your photon torpedoes no matter how much extra power Scotty gives you.

He asked to start.

But everything else about the game was great. The puzzles even managed to mostly avoid traditional adventure game logic, which was probably a side effect of being confined to the sciencey-science of Star Trek.

Then again, that also means you ran into the occasional ridiculously obtuse puzzle, like one where you had to convert Base 10 math to Base 3 math, which I guess was this game's version of Leisure Suit Larry's "Prove You're An Adult" quiz, but for nerds. Well, *nerdier* nerds, anyway.

#4 - Indiana Jones and the Fate of Atlantis

I looked forward to this Lucasfilm (which had now become LucasArts) game probably more than any other, including my beloved Monkey Island series. It was more Indy, which was always welcome in my Indiana Jones obsessed brain.

(Yes, I own a licensed Indy fedora. And a brown leather jacket. And a whip. Stop laughing.)

Everyone loves this game, and people are always citing it as the objectively best Indy game to date, which is kind of silly because The Last Crusade exists and is clearly the better game. Fate of Atlantis is by no means bad or anything, but everything it did, The Last Crusade did just a little bit better.

I'm pretty sure Fate of Atlantis was also the first game I bought on CD after finally getting a single speed CD-ROM drive, which means it was the first "talkie" adventure game I ever played, which is what they were called back when things like adding digitized sound to games was a huge deal. Some games did this with optional add-ons you could buy that were usually called Speech Packs. (They were basically precursors to the money-grubbing DLC we have today.)

One thing LucasArts established very early on was that they were going to actually spend time and money on working with actual voice actors rather than just getting the programmers' families to come in and record some dialog on the weekend.

It made a huge difference.

#3 - Wolfenstein 3D

I remember downloading the shareware version of Wolf3D from a local BBS back in '92. It was near the end of my junior year in high school, and the sysop of the Around The Clock BBS broke into chat after I dialed in, just to tell me about this amazing new game I had to try immediately and without delay. Refusing him was not an option.

Having played Castle Wolfenstein on my Apple][and remembering it as a really fun game, I headed over to the files section and started my download of Wolfenstein 3D Shareware. Then, I went and ate dinner. And watched some TV. And then went to school the next day, because these were the days of 1200 baud modems, noisy phone lines, and non-resumable file transfers. These things took time.

Lots of time.

Anyway, once I finally got my hands on it and installed the thing, I was hooked. I burned through the shareware levels and decided that I actually wanted to buy a copy. I'd never actually bought any shareware game before, seeing as how the demos were usually enough to warn me off of most of the crap that was out there, but Wolf3D was actually good. And I wanted more.

Unfortunately, my parents didn't feel the same way about putting a check in the mail or giving their credit card info to some unknown game studio they didn't care about, so I had to either wait until retail copies started showing up, or for the sysop of the BBS to buy it…and then make it available in the secret file section.

Misspent youth, guys. Misspent youth.

Sadly, the rest of the game didn't live up to those initial Shareware levels (which was often the case back in those days, when the best of the game was shoved to the front to convince people to buy it), but it was still a good time.

#2 - Ultima Underworld

This game really made me mad. It ran a lot slower than Wolfenstein 3D and had a much smaller view window! How could that even be possible?! Those guys at Origin just don't know how to program!

Then, I played it. And I slowly realized that there was a whole lot more going on in Ultima Underworld than there was in Wolf3D. I could look up and down, for starters. The graphics were also more detailed, with more textures and animation. Then there were the RPG stats, the combat, the magic system, NPCs, puzzles, etc...

It was Ultima, but underground. It was all those dungeons I'd crawled through years before in 1st person that looked like the scribbled line drawings of a coked-up four-year-old with an awful drug habit for a toddler, only this time it was in "real" 3D. I was hooked, and I couldn't stop playing it.

I'm still playing it. I go back to it every year or two, just to experience the Stygian Abyss all over again. And, thanks to the handy automap and full movement (as opposed to the stepped slideshows of, say, the Eye of the Beholder series), I can even manage to play it without getting lost and dying ALL THE TIME.

#1 - Ultima VII: The Black Gate

The perfect Ultima.

No game in the series before or (especially) after ever came as close to realizing a simulated world better than Ultima VII and it's kinda/sorta sequel, Ultima VII: Part Two: The Serpent Isle. The story was great, the Guardian was a terrific villain, and all my old friends were back, but it was the world that got me in U7.

You could cut down wheat and take it to a mill, where you could grind it into flour that you could then add water to and make dough, which you could then stick in an oven to make bread. And that was just one of the many things you could do in the game.

NPCs went about their business, independent of the player's presence. People had lives, the world had a schedule, and things mattered. Or they seemed to, at least. Which was good enough for me.

The only real downside to the game was the "realistic" way all the stuff in your backpack would jostle around as you walked, thereby making the three-pixel key you needed to find later a nearly impossible task.

Also, getting everyone to just sit the hell down in that infuriating wagon was a pain in my butt I've still not fully recovered from.

But everything else? AMAZING.

<u>1993</u>

#10 - Coaster

Another little-known title that I loved is once again from Disney Interactive. Coaster really kindled my deep love of the marriage of art and science that is the rollercoaster, and I'm still thankful to it for that. The things used to terrify me as a kid, mostly because I weighed negative pounds and always felt like I was one corkscrew away from sliding under the safety bar and plummeting to my untimely death.

That never happened, though. Spoilers.

I was never very good at this game, which is something I'm now realizing was kind of a common theme with me and the games of my youth. Still, I loved trying to make legitimate coasters that would thrill the crazy panel of judges assembled in this game. But it was freaking hard.

You designed your rollercoasters on what to my soon-to-be-a-high-school-graduate mind was a veritable fully-realized AutoCAD workstation, but was really just a simplified bit of trickery. The hardest part of any coaster design, though, was connecting the final bit of track to the station.

Which is probably a pretty crucial thing to get right if you want repeat customers, but it was so infuriating, I usually just gave up and made a simple track with impossible G-forces that would pretty much kill anyone who looked at it funny.

The judges were an odd assortment of little computer people who the game would pretend wanted to ride your coaster, and they all had different criteria they were interested in. The one I remember the most was the snot-nosed kid who just wanted whatever you'd spent hours making to be faster, scarier, and in every way more extreme than anything any of the other judges wanted. It was impossible to please them all, and it really made me hate that kid.

#9 - Space Quest V

The last Space Quest I played was also my favorite. I don't know exactly why SQ5 clicked with me, but it was probably because I was a huge space and Star Trek nerd, so it hit all the right parody notes rattling around inside my dusty braincase.

From cheating on my final exam at the Academy to doing time in the totally-not-the-millennium-falcon simulator, I loved every minute of it. Even the stupid fart joke every time Roger sat down in the captain's chair of his garbage scow made me giggle like I was 12 years old again.

I don't remember there being a single no-win state in the game, either. Which was kind of amazing, considering it was a Sierra title. It's probably the only real reason I was ever able to complete the thing, now that I think about it.

#8 - The 7th Guest / Dracula Unleashed

Okay, this one is a little bit of a cop-out, but I couldn't choose one of these games over the other. They were my first (and last) willing forays into the FMV-crazed world of the '90s (not counting Wing Commander 4 and one or two other misadventures in really bad videoland), and my memory of both of them really is a flat tie.

The 7th Guest had the cooler atmosphere, but the whole thing being more or less just Myst dressed up in a Halloween costume really put me off. I don't mind the occasional logic puzzle in an adventure game, but I don't want to play a whole game entirely composed of moving chess pieces around and dividing up slices of cake evenly between demon ghost people. I don't want to re-arrange soup cans in an obtuse word puzzle, and I absolutely hated how none of the puzzles ever told you what they wanted you to do, or even what the rules were.

Dracula Unleashed went the complete opposite route, had no logic puzzles at all, and was really just a choose-your-own-adventure VHS tape on a postage stamp-sized screen. It wasn't all that fun and was pretty much an awful soap opera filled with awful soap opera actors in awful soap opera makeup, but I sunk a ton of hours into it, just so I could be amazed by how my COMPUTER was playing a MOVIE.

We were easily amused back in those days.

#7 - Freddy Pharkas: Frontier Pharmacist

The second Sierra game to feature a lyrical song in the intro was also the second of any game to feature a lyrical song in the intro, the first being Conquests of the Longbow. This time, you followed a bouncing ball over the lyrics, just in case you weren't able to hear them in your head along the obvious melody. It worked, though.

The game itself is really, really short, but it was probably Al Lowe's best game. It still has some of his trademark puerile humor, like when the town is overcome by a noxious cloud of horse farts, but most of it is solid, clever dialog in a setting we've always seen too little of in gaming: the old west.

Saying too much about the plot would spoil the few surprises it has in store, but it's still entirely playable today and is as fun as it ever was. My favorite part was when the game actually let me be a pharmacist, which is also how it worked in its copy protection. The manual had a list of ailments along with their appropriate cures, which you then had to prepare in Freddy's little laboratory according to the instructions provided. It was one of the better uses of manual-as-copy-protection, and making all the little pills and elixirs for the townsfolk was a lot of fun.

They really could've just made an entire game around that one mechanic. I'd have played it.

#6 - Gabriel Knight: Sins of the Fathers

One of the last Sierra games that will show up on this list is this one, the first Gabriel Knight game. The series took a nosedive into crappy FMV after the first game, followed by crappy 3D after that and never quite recovered from either, but the first game still holds up.

(Okay, the FMV in the second game wasn't all that awful. It was actually some of the better video in gaming at the time. Still, it was full motion video and, even when done well, it kinda always sucked.)

It's devoid of most of the negative trappings of Sierra games, although by this time, they were making CD versions of most of their games, which meant they had voiceovers usually done by whoever wasn't busy working on categorizing their nose mucus according to booger viscosity that day. Gabriel Knight actually had real voice talent though, even if traditional actors hadn't quite figured out how to do VO for a game yet.

Which probably explains why Tim Curry was an awful Gabriel Knight. I love the guy, but he didn't sound anything at all like either someone from the Deep South or a New Orleans native. Here's a tip, Hollywood people and game devs: New Orleans natives don't sound like they're from Gone With the Wind. The New Orleans accent is a whole lot closer to a New England one than it is to the typical drawl-ridden caricature of the typical southern accent, which itself is usually a take on a Savannah, Georgia accent that has about as much to do with how people in the rest of the South sound as the characters from Fargo.

On the plus side, the game is filled with voodoo and mystery, and they even managed to get most of the locations right. Or at least sufficiently recognizable as background art. They remastered it recently, too. I'd recommend the original over the remaster, but hey. You do you.

Paddle whatever floats your pirogue, sha.

#5 - Sam & Max Hit the Road

I've never loved this game as much as everyone else seems to love this game. It was fun enough, but it always seemed like it was trying just a bit too hard to be different or whatever. I don't know; it's an intangible thing.

Maybe I just didn't dig the sideshow vibe or the road trip aesthetic, but something about it just never really clicked with me. It was good enough for 1993, had some great art and animation, and I still played it from beginning to end and even chuckled at most of the jokes along the way - but if I ever had to rate my top ten adventure games of all time, it probably wouldn't make the list.

I know. I'm the worst.

#4 - Ultima Underworld II

Taking place after the events of Ultima VII, UU2 was more of the same from Ultima Underworld...but a LOT more of it. There were more characters, more locations, more puzzles, and even more world to discover and explore, thanks to a faceted Blackrock gem in Lord British's basement. There were even the internal drama-plagued politics of British's castle to manage, with things like preventing (or encouraging) a worker's revolt and stuff.

It had a lot more going for it than UU1, but it lost some of the original's charm along the way. I'm not sure if it had more to do with me getting older, or maybe I was just getting burned out on dungeon crawlers, or maybe the dang game was just too big - but I never finished it.

And I've never really wanted to, either.

Weird.

143

#3 - Doom

There's a reason this game launched a genre, and that's because it's ridiculously fun. It's tightly designed, has great enemies, satisfying weapons, smart levels and AI bad guys who can annoy each other until they spend more time trying to murder one another in the shotguns than they do aiming their death barrels at your face.

Doom improved on Wolfenstein in every way. It brought dynamic lighting to the table, for example, so you could run into a fully lit room with a lot of ammo and the big, shiny key you needed sitting on a pedestal, and just know that picking it up was going to turn out the lights and unleash hell. Literally.

But even more than its single-player campaign of shooting monster demon murderbots in the face with shotguns was shooting your friends in their faces with shotguns, because Doom introduced multiplayer to the world, which changed everything.

LAN parties suddenly became a thing. You'd drag your giant PC over to a friend's house, where you'd meet up with several other friends who were all dragging their giant PCs, too. Then, you'd spend an hour hooking everything up through either a crappy Ethernet hub or ridiculous BNC connections, and another hour getting all the computers talking to each other. But then – eventually – you would launch the game and meet your friends on the battlefield.

And it was glorious.

Pizza, soda, chips, friends, and Doom were all any self-respecting geek needed over a weekend, and Deathmatches quickly became regular after-hours affairs at many a workplace. Doom was everywhere, and if you weren't playing it in '93, then you either knew someone who was or you hadn't been born yet.

If you want a taste of how Doom made you feel when it was new but you weren't around at the time, go download a copy of Brutal Doom. It's much crazier than the original ever was, but it *feels* more *now* like Doom felt *then*, if that makes any sense.

#2 - Day of the Tentacle

DOTT narrowly missed my #1 spot for this year. It probably would've made it to the top, if someone had bothered to allow the CD-ROM version to BUFFER THE COMMON SOUND EFFECTS. Or maybe at least install them to the hard drive.

I have no complaints about Day of the Tentacle as a game. As a game, I love it. It's perfect. The art style showed what you could accomplish with great art direction and true mastery over Deluxe Paint. The writing was top shelf, and the voice acting was great. The puzzles were fun and funny.

But those dang sound effects...

See, I had a single-speed CD-ROM drive back in '93, just like a lot of people. This meant it was painfully slow to seek out information from the shiny plastic Phantasm discs, which translated to incredibly annoying - and lengthy - pauses every time it had to stop whatever it was doing to go load up the sound effect of, say, purple tentacle's suction cup sloshing along the ground.

Every. Single. Time. It. Happened.

Buffering the sound files would've fixed that. Loading them onto the hard drive would've fixed it, too. But noooo. I had to go buy a double-speed drive JUST TO PLAY DAY OF THE TENTACLE.

Which I loved, but that oversight cost it the gold.

As for the game itself, there's really nothing bad I could say about it (other than the whole sound file thing), even if I wanted to. Great puzzles, multiple characters just like the first Maniac Mansion, and more jokes and genuine laughs than any game I'd played before.

They even remastered it recently, so you have no excuse for not playing it.

So go play it.

Seriously.

#1 - Star Wars: X-Wing

X-Wing was a space combat simulator set in the Star Wars universe that allowed me to pretend I was in the Rebel Alliance, which was more or less everything I ever wanted video games to be.

I had long debates with a couple of friends over whether Wing Commander was better than X-Wing, and in my mind, they always lost. Sure, WC had more cinematic flair, but it was an arcade game. X-Wing was a simulator, with power management and locking s-foils in attack positions and other crap.

I played the hell out of this game, much more than I played either Wing Commander 1 or 2. And I didn't just play it, either. I *pretended* while I played it, which is something I'm rarely able to do in a game anymore. But while I was playing X-Wing, I could make believe I was actually inside that cockpit. I was really pew pewing my lasers at TIE fighters. I was really the best hope for the Rebel Alliance.

I really was Luke Freaking Skywalker!

It was glorious.

About the Author

Kristian Bland is an Editor, Indefatigable Stepdad, and Inventor of Nothing Useful. He also writes sometimes, including this About page, which makes him feel weird because he's talking about himself in the third person like some kind of lunatic.

He's written a few of other books: *A Trick of Light and Shadow*, *A Lifetime of Questionable Decisions*, and *Naked* Shingle, which you should totally check out if you haven't already.

Okay, he's gonna stop writing about himself now. It's just too weird, y'all.

"Be excellent to each other."
-Wyld Stallyns

www.ingramcontent.com/pod-product-compliance
Lightning Source LLC
Chambersburg PA
CBHW041429050326
40690CB00002B/472

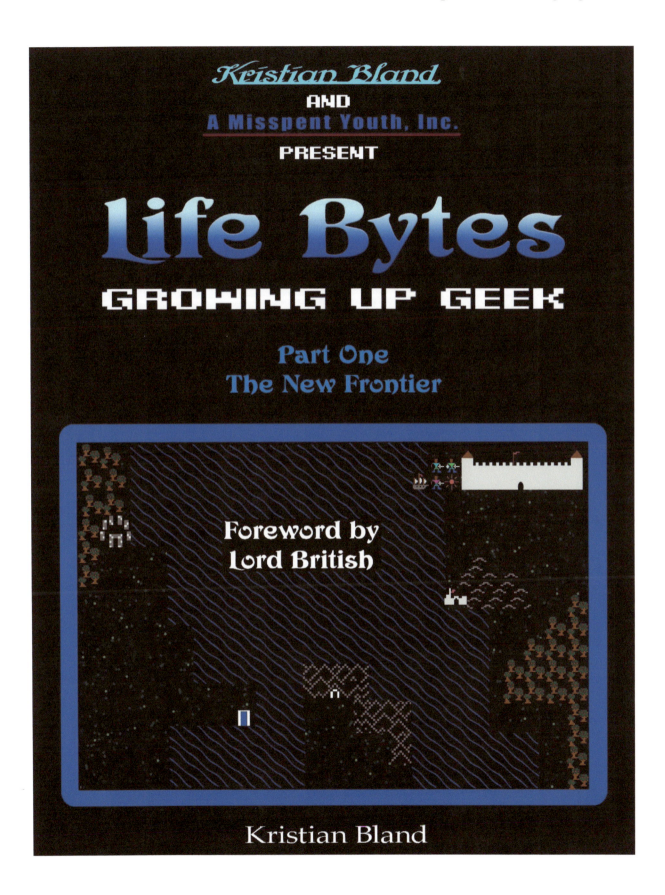

Kristian Bland AND A Misspent Youth, Inc. PRESENT

Life Bytes

GROWING UP GEEK

Part One
The New Frontier

Foreword by
Lord British

Kristian Bland

Additional Books by Kristian Bland

A Trick of Light and Shadow
A Lifetime of Questionable Decisions
Naked Shingles
Life Bytes: Growing Up Geek series